Laura Svedberg-Roker
gave me this book
after Ethics class
of 1991-1992

From Survival to the Universe

Eugene W. Mathes

From Survival to the Universe

Values and Psychological Well-Being

Nelson-Hall nh Chicago

Library of Congress Cataloging in Publication Data

Mathes, Eugene W.
From survival to the universe.

Bibliography: p.
Includes index.
1. Values. 2. Mental health. I. Title.
BF778.M33 170'.42 81-9583
ISBN 0-88229-595-0 (cloth) AACR2
ISBN 0-88229-790-2 (paper)

Manufactured in the United States of America

10 9 8 7 6 5 4 3 2 1

To my parents who gave me a deep concern for values and
Daniel Bergman who introduced me to psychology

Contents

Preface

Let me begin by discussing the basic purpose of this book. I am proposing a theory of values that makes sense out of the bits and pieces of empirical data dealing with values. The theory of values presented here deals with two aspects of human experience. One aspect is the relationship of human beings to their selves. It deals with the good life, the life that produces pleasure and avoids pain, the life that leads to happiness and peace of mind. It is the life that each individual should live in order to get the most out of staying on this earth. The second aspect involves relationships with other people. It deals with morality and ethics, how an individual should treat others. Although we have been brought up to separate these two areas of experience and have been taught that they are independent of each other and even inversely related (for example, we have sayings like "conscience is that which hurts when everything else feels so good") I have found that this is not true. The data seem to suggest that these two aspects of human experience are highly related. The happy individual is also the ethical individual, and the good life is also the moral life. For this reason, pleasure, pain, and morality are not dealt with separately, but instead within a single theoretical framework.

A Text on Psychological Adjustment

After having written the first draft of this book, I discovered that I had accomplished a second objective. I had written a textbook on the psychology of adjustment. I found that I had included in the book almost all of the material that I usually present in my adjustment class. Although I may be accused of having placed my adjustment lectures into the book as a filler, I do not believe that this is true. Logically, the happy and ethical life is synonymous with the well-adjusted and psychologically healthy life; thus, a theory of values is also a theory of adjustment and vice versa. In writing the final draft of this book, I have taken special care to write at a level so that anyone who has had an introductory course in psychology can understand it. Therefore, it can be used as an undergraduate textbook in psychology of adjustment courses.

As a textbook on adjustment it differs from other textbooks on adjustment in that it does not take either the approach of the personality theorists or of the problems theorists. It does not first describe Freud's ideas about psychological health and then contradict them with the ideas of Carl Rogers, and finally contradict the theories of both Freud and Rogers with those of B. F. Skinner. Nor does it deal with helplessness apart from anxiety and depression, or identity apart from intimacy and love. Instead, I have attempted to create a single theory that integrates all of the adjustment data (and quite a bit of additional data) into a single whole.

A Science of Values?

To further introduce this book, let me describe the history of its development. As an undergraduate I learned in my introductory philosophy class (or possibly in my ethics class) that scientists can only deal with "that which is." They cannot deal with "that which ought to be." That is, they can deal with facts, but not values. This notion was further reinforced in graduate school, where I soon discovered that discussions of research design, multivariate analysis of variance, and the literature on short-term memory, cognitive dissonance, and nonverbal communication were encouraged, but discussions of religion and philosophy (values) were viewed as weird and unworthy of a person who wished to become a scientist in the field of psychology. I also learned about J. B. Watson, the George Washington of psychology, who freed psychology from the domination of philosophy. Watson freed psychology so that it could take its rightful place alongside the sciences of biology, physics, and chemistry, the sciences that were doing so much to make the world a more comfortable place in which to live. So throughout my undergraduate and graduate years I believed that psychologists could devise numerous procedures for modifying their own and other people's behavior, but that they could not determine, empirically, the purposes to which these methods should be put. For example, they could devise therapies for restoring potency to heterosexuals and homosexuals, therapies for making homosexuals into heterosexuals and heterosexuals into bisexuals, and therapies for rendering child molesters and rapists impotent, but they could not define healthy sexual behavior. Such decisions were to be left to professional committees on ethics, political assemblies, priests, rabbis, and ministers, and often, chance.

Only after I had graduated from school and had time to pursue my own interests did I begin to seriously doubt the separation of science and values. It seemed to me that when psychologists did research on psychological health, they were empirically studying values, even though they were not using the language of values. In studying psychological health they were studying the good life, the life individuals *should* live. In my second year of teaching I read Abraham Maslow's (1972) book, *The Farther Reaches of Human Nature,* and was delighted to find his statement that values are organismic, that is, rooted in biology, and as such can be scientifically studied. I subsequently read two articles in *American Psychologist,* a journal of the American Psychological Association, that argued that the empirical study of values is possible. The first was by Jerome Frank, "Nature and Functions of Belief Systems: Humanism and Transcendental Religion" (1977), and the other was by R. W. Sperry, "Bridging Science and Values: A Unifying View of Mind and Brain" (1977). As a result, I was convinced that the empirical study of values was possible. I also felt, however, that no worthwhile research about values had yet been carried out. I believed that a psychology of values was a thing of the future and a book on values was not yet possible.

The immediate impetus for writing this book came from a different source. Last summer I taught a class on humanistic psychology, and as an exercise, I had the students list the goals they wished to achieve before they died. One girl stated that, among other things, she wanted to own a monkey and write two books. I was highly impressed by the goal of "two books." Although I had obtained a Ph.D. and written a number of professional articles, I had never had the courage to write one book, let alone two. I mentioned this incident to a colleague, and he suggested that we swear, right there and then, to write two books, even though they might not be published. The rest of the summer I read books and articles, thought, scribbled, and struggled, trying to write my first book. Somehow, then, everything fell into place, and this book on values resulted. I discovered that empirical data on values was not something new, but it had been accumulating since the first empirical studies were carried out on human behavior. What was required, however, was that the existing data be looked at in a new way. This book is an attempt to interpret the data on values that psychologists have been generating over the past century or so.

Acknowledgments

Several people have helped me greatly in writing this book. I would like to thank Lois Gerson and Jim Garrett for encouraging me to write the book, and I would also like to thank the students at Western Illinois University whom I have taught over the past five years. Interacting with them helped to generate much of the material found here. Finally, I would like to thank Susan Matthys, who proofread the manuscript, Mablene Weaver and the secretaries of Western's Dean of Arts and Sciences, who typed it, and my dog, Willie, who gave me moral support while I carried out the arduous task of carving out the various drafts of this book.

1. The Empirical Study of Values

Although a number of strategies can be followed in the empirical study of values, probably the easiest approach is simply to ask people what they value. This is the approach that has frequently been used by anthropologists studying other cultures and by political scientists, sociologists, and social psychologists conducting opinion polls and attitude surveys. According to this strategy, the "good" consists of the values that most people say are important. In living, one should try as much as possible to conform to the values of the majority of the inhabitants of this world.

The Polling Approach to Studying Values

A major problem with the polling approach, however, is that people value a tremendously wide variety of things. Almost every object, behavior, feeling, and idea has been valued by a group of people at some time. Headhunting has been valued by tribes of the Philippines, cannibalism by tribes living in New Guinea, scalp-taking by American Indians, dueling by eighteenth-century Europeans, and suicide by the Japanese. Most Americans value monogamy, whereas Arab shieks are famous for their harems, and a few tribes in India practice (or practiced) polyandry. In the United States, divorce used to be a sin, but now it is common. In Victorian England, women tried to cover themselves almost entirely; during the same period in India, however, the woman who covered her breasts was considered immoral, a prostitute. Bull-, cock-, and people-fighting and dog-, horse-, and frog-racing have all been engaged in for entertainment at different times and places. It seems inappropriate to simply average all of these data.

Although the diverse and contradictory nature of the values endorsed by human beings poses a serious problem for the polling approach, this problem could probably be overcome by a system of classification or the creation of a theory of values. The polling approach, however, has another flaw that I consider fatal: the average, by definition, cannot be the best. An IQ of 130 or 140 is preferable to an average IQ of 100, and never being sick is preferable to being sick a few days out of each year, which is what the average individual must endure. Although living by the values of the majority would almost always protect people from making foolish or disastrous choices, it would also prevent them from ever doing anything truly exceptional, noble, or great. Furthermore, striving for the average would eventually eliminate all exploration and change. Progress would cease, and the world would stagnate.

Maslow's Modified Polling Approach

If we give up the polling approach, what other strategies are available? One variation of this approach has been developed by Abraham Maslow (1972), who suggested that only the values of superior people be polled. In this way ones does not discover the average, but only the best. Maslow (1970b) derived this strategy by conducting an experiment in which chickens were allowed to eat whatever they wanted for a given period of time. During this time, daily records were kept of what each chicken ate in addition to its weight, egg production, and so on. After the initial period the records were examined, and the chickens were divided into inferior and superior groups by factors such as weight and egg production, for example. During the second part of the experiment, all of the chickens were fed the diet selected by the superior chickens. As a result, the inferior group increased rapidly in weight, egg production, and so on, although they never quite equaled the superior group. In this experiment the superior chickens were "asked" what they valued for food, and when the inferior chickens were forced to conform to these values, it was found that they became better chickens.

Using the same logic Maslow spent the latter part of his life interviewing superior people, that is, people whom he called "self-actualizing," asking them what they valued. He found that all of them valued a group of values that he called "metavalues," which include truth, goodness, beauty, unity (wholeness), dichotomy-transcendence, aliveness (process), uniqueness, perfection, necessity, completion (finality), justice, order, simplicity, richness (totality and comprehensiveness), effortlessness, playfulness, self-sufficiency, and meaningfulness. Maslow felt the metavalues constituted the ultimate good and suggested that everyone be educated to follow them.

Although I personally like Maslow's list of metavalues and believe that they have a certain validity (Mathes, 1978), I am unhappy with the strategy that Maslow followed in finding them. His strategy seems circular. In selecting superior people, Maslow depended primarily upon his intuition rather than an objective criterion. Most likely Maslow believed in metavalues even before conducting his research, and in selecting superior people, he selected people who also believed in metavalues. Consequently, when he asked them what they valued, he got the answer he wanted—metavalues. This kind of research proves nothing. If Maslow had liked child molesting, murder, rape, and incest, his superior (self-actualizing) people would have included Charles Manson, Adolf Hitler, and select members of the Hell's Angels and the Ku Klux Klan. Under these circumstances he would have discovered that the good consists of child molesting, murder, rape, and incest. It is not that his theory is wrong, it is just that his method of proving it was inadequate.

I am also somewhat suspicious of Maslow's plan to educate average and inferior individuals to follow metavalues even though they would prefer to live by other values. This plan smells a bit like fascism or brainwashing.

Kohlberg's Developmental Approach to the Study of Values

A third strategy, and one that I find most satisfying, is Lawrence Kohlberg's (1976) developmental approach. Kohlberg suggests that people's values change as a result of maturation and experience and that this change is orderly. Everyone starts with value A and then moves to B, and from there moves through C, D, E, and so on. Although certain people go through the sequence faster and reach a further point in the sequence than others, the sequence is fixed. Value development is similar to development in other areas, for example, locomotion. Babies initially squirm about, going nowhere, then they learn to "swim" over the floor on their bellies. This is followed by crawling, toddling, walking, and finally running. Some people go through this sequence faster than others, and some people never complete the entire sequence. The order, however, is fixed; no one walks before toddling or runs before crawling. In studying values, Kohlberg suggests that the sequence of value stages individuals go through as they develop be determined by empirical research.

This approach is better than that of polling in that the idea of superior and inferior values is maintained, although not in a malicious way. Values that appear later in the development sequence are considered superior to those that appeared earlier in the same way that walking is considered superior to crawling. Kohlberg's strategy also provides a theoretical framework for classifying the vast amounts of data that exist on values and may explain some of the apparent contradictions found in the data.

Furthermore, the developmental approach is superior to Maslow's in that it is not circular. It follows Maslow's strategy of finding the ultimate good by asking superior people, but it avoids the trap of circularity by defining superiority in developmental terms. Superiority is operationally defined in terms of age, physical and mental maturity, experience, and so on, variables that are conceptually independent of values. Kohlberg's strategy has another advantage—it is not authoritarian. Kohlberg does not recommend that adult values be forced on children. Whatever an individual values at a given time is what is considered appropriate. Everyone has to value the things two-year-olds value before they can value the things that are valued by a gray-haired sage. Kohlberg does not, however, advocate total anarchy. Experiences that facilitate development should be encouraged, whereas those that interfere with value development should be avoided. In the next chapter I shall use Kohlberg's strategy to create a theory of values.

2. Value Development

In the previous chapter it was proposed that the most effective approach to the empirical study of values is the developmental approach suggested by Kohlberg. Kohlberg, as it was noted, suggested that an individual's values develop in an orderly sequence as a result of maturation and experience, and he proposed that this sequence be explored by empirical observation. Three theorists have been concerned with value development. They are Maslow (1970a), Erik Erikson (1963), and Kohlberg (1976) himself. In this chapter I plan to review the observations of these three men and then attempt to show how they point to a common developmental value sequence.

Maslow's Hierarchy of Needs

Maslow (1970a) suggests that human development involves learning how to regularly satisfy five classes of needs that form the following hierarchy: physiological (most basic), safety, belongingness, esteem, and self-actualization. Needs lower in the hierarchy are prepotent to needs higher in the hierarchy, which means that lower needs must be satisfied before needs higher in the hierarchy can emerge. Thus the primary concerns of newborn infants center around eating, sleeping, breathing, defecating, and staying warm and dry. Only after they acquire the skills needed to satisfy their physiological needs can infants become interested in safety. If individuals never learn how to satisfy their physiological needs, as is the case with the proverbial starving millions in India and China, their safety needs never emerge.

Acquiring safety involves developing attitudes of courage and endurance, acquiring information and skills, and working out arrangements whereby long-range survival is secured. People who are concerned with safety are similar to people who are concerned with physiological needs in that both are interested in eating, sleeping, and so on. They differ, however, in that people functioning at the physiological level are concerned only with immediate physiological satisfaction, whereas people functioning at the safety level are concerned with the satisfaction of their physiological needs not only now but also in the future. They are concerned with long-term survival, and for example, they may store grain, obtain inoculations, put money in the bank, and take out medical insurance.

Once people feel secure about their future survival, belongingness needs emerge, that is, they become lonely. They become interested in making friends and joining various groups. After people acquire friends and are no longer lonely, they become concerned with the accomplishment of significant tasks so that they can earn the admiration of others as well as themselves. In other words, esteem needs arise. Once people have assembled noteworthy achievements and developed skills by which future achievements are more or less assured, they are ready to self-actualize.

Self-Actualization

Self-actualization is unique from the four levels of needs just discussed because it does not involve the satisfaction of needs. All of the needs that can be experienced by human beings can be classified as physiological, safety, belongingness, or esteem needs. Self-actualizing people are in an "ideal" state in which nothing presses them from within or without. They are complete. They cannot think of anything more that they need. As a result, self-actualizing people see things and people as they really are rather than as means to ends. For example, hungry people see others as meal tickets, objects from which to panhandle quarters; insecure people see others as protectors who will kiss their wounds and make everything all right; lonely people see others as lovers who will sweep them off their feet and pledge undying devotion; and ambitious people see others as admirers, stepping stones, and competitors. Self-actualizing people, however, see other people as they actually are in their entirety.

Metavalues

Although self-actualizing people have no needs, this does not mean that they are inactive. Most often they are highly involved in a task or calling that they greatly enjoy and that is also of great importance to humanity. Although the task is not a means by which their deficiency needs are satisfied (that is, physiological, safety, belongingness, and esteem needs), neither is it an end in itself. Instead, it is a means whereby metavalues are actualized. Although Maslow does not specify how metavalues differ from other values, he does provide a partial list of such values. This list, which has already been presented in the first chapter, includes truth, goodness, beauty, unity (wholeness), dichotomy-transcendence, aliveness (process), uniqueness, perfection, necessity, completion (finality), justice, order, simplicity, richness (totality and comprehensiveness), effortlessness, playfulness, self-sufficiency, and meaningfulness.

Actualizing metavalues involves production rather than consumption, with the result that the selfishness-altruism dichotomy is transcended. That is, in actualizing metavalues people are both totally selfish and totally altruistic. Consequently, when the self-actualizing painter paints a picture to increase the amount of beauty in the world, the painter not only enjoys the painting but everyone who views it also enjoys it. Likewise, when the self-actualizing scientist performs an experiment to increase the amount of truth available to humankind (for example, Fleming's experiments with penicillin), the scientist enjoys the discovery but everyone else benefits as well. In satisfying deficiency needs this is not true. If I have a candy bar I can either eat it or give it to someone else but I cannot both eat it and give it away. If I have $100 I can either buy insurance for my car or for someone else's car but not for both cars. If I have a girl friend, I can either marry her or someone else can marry her, but both of us cannot marry her (and have her totally). Whenever a race is run, election held, or art competition judged there is only one winner. If I win, then you cannot, and vice versa. In dealing with deficiency needs, selfishness and altruism are incompatible. People are either selfish or altruistic but never both at the same time.

Maslow believed that metavalues are organismically based, that is, grounded in biology; they are, therefore, not only appropriate topics for scientific investigation but also universal. Cultures can be judged either good or bad depending on whether or not they facilitate the satisfaction of metavalues. Maslow's theory of metavalues is not compatible with cultural relativism, which states that no values higher than a culture's own values exist.

Although little formal research has been carried out testing Maslow's theory of value evolution (see Mathes, 1978; Mathes and Edwards, 1978), this does not mean that the theory is not empirical. I believe that Maslow was an astute observer of human behavior and thus did not spin his theory out of nothing. It is grounded in his observations. Even so, further research of a more formal nature is needed to place it on a firmer empirical foundation.

Erikson's Developmental Stages

Erikson (1963, 1968) suggests that development involves the sequential acquisition of eight different values: trust, autonomy, initiative, industry, identity, intimacy, generativity, and ego-integrity. To achieve any given value, all earlier values must have been successfully attained.

Trust

The task facing newborn infants during the first year of life is achievement of a sense of trust in themselves, other people, and the world. Since newborn infants are helpless, whether or not they achieve this goal largely depends upon the people who are taking care of them. If these caretakers make certain that the needs of the infants are met (for example, that they do not go too long without milk, their diaper being changed, or being tickled and cuddled), they will conclude that people are okay and that the world is a good place in which to live. They will also conclude that they are worthwhile. Because parents treat their children well, they will be happy to be alive. On the other hand, if parents do not like their children and communicate this by neglecting their needs, ignoring their cries when they are distressed, and subjecting them to unnecessary discomforts, children will conclude that they are intolerable and that the world is a hostile place. They will develop a sense of mistrust and spend the rest of their lives protecting themselves from the world and running away from people.

Autonomy

Once children have achieved a sense of trust, they are ready to acquire autonomy. This stage of development takes place during the second and third years of life. During this stage children assert their will. The explore their environment and assume partial control over their destiny. They crawl and walk everywhere. When possible, they force their will onto others and do their best to prevent others from forcing their wills onto them. Two-year-olds are called "terrible" for good reason, and yet parents should delight in this terribleness, for it means that ultimately the children will be able to take care of themselves. To help children successfully acquire a sense of autonomy, parents should respect the individuality and wishes of each child. They should also, however, place realistic limitations on the freedom of the children. Although children believe that they are the center of the universe and that others were created to be their servants, this is not true. Perpetuating this illusion by spoiling children is not doing them a service. If the parents become upset when children assert their own will, perceiving them as ungrateful and harshly putting them down, they will fail in this stage of development. They will conclude that asserting their will is bad and develop feelings of shame and doubt. They will be dependent on other people for the rest of their lives. Paradoxically, learning to depend on other people, the first developmental task, is a prerequisite to the second developmental task, learning to be independent.

Initiative

After children have acquired a sense of autonomy, they are ready to achieve initiative. The autonomy that children acquire during their second and third years is combined with sexual curiosity during their fourth and fifth years to produce highly active little individuals. To harness this almost random activity, children must acquire a conscience; they must internalize the rules of cooperative living. They have to learn to play fair, share, and tell the truth and learn not to hurt others, steal, or break things. Although acquiring a conscience limits the freedom of children for selfish indulgence, it nevertheless increases their freedom for social involvement. A conscience will keep children from stealing their friends' toys, and it provides them with the social skills necessary for sharing their toys. Not only does a conscience make social interaction possible, but it also facilitates control over the environment. A conscience helps children control their impulsiveness so they can delay gratification and achieve long-range goals. Parents, older brothers and sisters, and teachers who are either too strict or too lenient with children will cause them to fail this stage. If the socializers are too severe, children will acquire a conscience that is too strict and will feel guilty about everything they do. They will be unable to take initiative for fear that they will do something wrong. On the other hand, if the socializers are too lenient, children will not develop a conscience at all. Children who lack a conscience will be impulsive and asocial and will probably end up in prison as adults.

Industry

Once children have acquired an effective conscience, they are ready to achieve a sense of industry. Industry, which is acquired during the grade-school years, involves learning the basic skills necessary for making children productive members of their culture. They must learn how to tie their shoestrings, say the pledge of allegiance to the flag, write their name, count, and read books. They have to learn about Jesus, Columbus, Lincoln, Kennedy, Indians, the continents of the world, and Sputnik, and how to eat a balanced meal and run a paper route. In our society these skills are learned, for the most part, in school. Success in school leads to a sense of industry while failure leads to feelings of inferiority.

Identity

After industry people must acquire a sense of personal identity. Identity achievement occurs during adolescence. Although having an identity is not unique to adolescents and adults, the identity of adolescents and adults differs from that of children in that it is chosen instead of given. While children have identities that consist of the cluster of characteristics that make them unique from other children, the children did not choose these characteristics. When I was eight I lived at 1114 Peace Street, Pella, Iowa, was in the fourth grade, and had a pony named Exie. I did not, however, choose these characteristics. I lived on Peace Street because my parents lived there, attended the fourth grade because I was eight years old, and had Exie because someone had given her to my father. During adolescence, teenagers are given choices about education, career, ideological commitments, residence, and friends; in making these choices, they create their identities. During my adolescence I chose to follow evangelical Christianity, to go to Central College, to follow philosophical naturalism (a little later), and to major in psychology, and in so doing I was creating my own identity. In this manner I took charge of and became responsible for my own destiny. It takes courage to achieve a sense of personal identity because decision making is difficult. When people make their own choices and these choices turn out poorly, they can blame no one but themselves. Because identity achievement is fraught with difficulties, many individuals avoid it by refusing to make choices. They have parents, peers, a friend, or chance make the decisions for them. If people abdicate their responsibility in this manner, they will be left with the feeling that they really do not know who they are, that they are simply playing a series of disconnected roles. Erikson calls this state role diffusion.

Intimacy

Intimacy follows identity. Once people have found (or formed) themselves, they want to fall in love. They want to find someone with whom they can make love, someone to whom they can show care and devotion, someone who reciprocates their confidences, erotic love, and caring. Commitment is an important part of intimacy. True intimacy (love) always involves a quality of "till death do us part." The attainment of intimacy usually takes place during young adulthood. Failure to find someone to love results in isolation and loneliness.

Generativity

People who have attained intimacy are ready for generativity, which involves relating to the world and the people that inhabit it through work and love. During this period people are most productive in their jobs, and also during this period people have children. Unlike previous stages of development, at this stage people pour most of their resources into the growth of their children, rather than their own growth. Although most people attain generativity by having children, this end can be achieved through any activity that is oriented toward the nurturing of the next generation. Developing solar energy, teaching kindergarten, or manufacturing educational toys are examples of alternative methods. Failure to achieve generativity leads to stagnation and boredom. Housewives who spend their days painting their fingernails and watching soap operas are not to be envied over mothers who are "burdened" with the drudgery of feeding babies and changing their diapers; rather, they are to be pitied.

Ego-Integrity

The last task to be accomplished is ego-integrity. Ego-integrity takes place during late adulthood and involves reviewing one's life and feeling contentment with it. People who have successfully completed all of the previous tasks will have this sense of contentment, a satisfied mind. They will feel that they have lived their lives well, that they have experienced everything that life has to offer, and that they have done everything that they were supposed to do. People like this do not fear death but rather welcome it. They have lived their lives completely and are ready for them to end. People who have not succeeded in accomplishing all of the developmental tasks fear old age and death. They still have things to accomplish, and yet time has run out.

Such people experience a great deal of bitterness and despair and often violently resist death.

This is Erikson's theory of value development. Like Maslow's theory, it has resulted primarily from clinical observation and requires more systematic research.

Kohlberg's Theory of Moral Development

Kohlberg's (1976) theory concerns moral development. It differs from the theories of Maslow and Erikson in that it focuses primarily on how people relate to other people rather than on how people provide for their own happiness. Kohlberg suggests that moral development involves three broad levels, each with two substages. The first level is the preconventional level, and it is made up of the substages (1) heteronomous morality and (2) individualism, instrumental purpose, and exchange. The second level is the conventional level, and it is made up of the substages (3) mutual interpersonal expectations, relationships, and interpersonal conformity and (4) social system and conscience. The third level is the postconventional or principled morality level and is composed of the substages (5) social contract or utility and individual rights and (6) universal ethical principles. Newborn infants begin at Stage 1 and progress through the other stages as a result of cognitive development and experience. A higher stage of development cannot be attained without having completed the previous stages.

Heteronomous Morality

Preconventional individuals are essentially amoral. They are concerned only with their own happiness and either ignore other people or use them for their own ends. They are simple hedonists, avoiding anything that gives them pain and pursuing only that which gives them pleasure. The first preconventional substage of moral development, the heteronomous stage, involves doing whatever is necessary to avoid pain and punishment. This is the morality of newborn infants. Having just entered the world and being very small and helpless, their primary concern is with survival, that is, avoiding noxious stimuli that might destroy them. They are concerned with avoiding hunger, stomach gas, loud noises, and blows to their bodies. At this point they are not yet interested in pleasure and spend most of their time sleeping when they are not in pain. No adults live at this level except possibly those who have been placed in concentration camps in which their survival is constantly under threat (see Bettelheim, 1943; Frankl, 1973).

Individualism, Instrumental Purpose, and Exchange

The second preconventional stage, individualism, instrumental purpose, and exchange, involves doing whatever is necessary to satisfy individual needs. It is a positive hedonism in which people are actively concerned with attaining pleasure. When rules must be followed to obtain positive benefits, they are followed. Thus, children will not cheat at marbles so that they will be allowed to play. If they do cheat, they make sure that they do not get caught. When a social exchange is necessary to obtain good outcomes, the exchange is carried out. For example, they will scratch someone else's back in order to receive a back scratching. Charlie Manson and his family functioned primarily at this stage as they enjoyed their orgies of sex, drugs, and, later, murder. Children enter this stage of moral development when their survival is no longer precarious.

Mutual Interpersonal Expectations, Relationships, and Interpersonal Conformity

Conventional morality involves a concern for the welfare of other people. Persons functioning at this level have acquired empathy skills and a conscience, and as a result, they are no longer totally self-centered. The first substage of conventional morality, mutual interpersonal expectations, relationships, and interpersonal conformity, involves behaving in such a way that people are liked by their family and friends. Empathy is necessary to reach this stage of development. If children cannot put themselves in the shoes of others, they cannot know how to please others. If they do not know how to please others, they will not be liked. Persons functioning at this level work in terms of the golden rule. They do unto others as they would have others do unto them. For example, they do not squeal on their friends because they know that they would not want their friends to tattle on them.

Social System and Conscience

The second substage of conventional morality, social system and conscience, involves maintaining law and order. It is an authoritarian and ethnocentric morality in which people view the laws and norms of their society as fixed. It is believed that disobeying the laws and norms will lead to dire consequences. Right action is action that is oriented toward following orders, doing one's duty, and maintaining the status quo. A well-developed conscience is necessary for functioning at this stage of moral development. The rules of society must be internalized so that people experience anxiety and guilt if they violate them. Morality at the fourth stage is a redneck, Archie Bunker kind of morality. The ethnocentrism of this stage of morality is found in slogans like, "America: Love her or leave her," and the practice of sending missionaries to other cultures to "save" them by teaching them to wear underwear and speak English. Individuals who violate cultural norms, like Communists, homosexuals, and hippies, are seen as a serious threat, and it is thus believed that they should be destroyed. Although stage 4 morality is usually associated with conventional behavior, there is no one-to-one relationship between the two. Many rednecks are hidden under long hair. "Freaks" who do not tolerate other people who do not smoke marijuana, live on vegetables, and enjoy free sex are probably also functioning at the social system and conscience level of morality.

Social Contract or Utility and Individual Rights

Principled or postconventional morality transcends the rules of a given culture and views morality in terms of all of humanity. It rises above the ethnocentrism of conventional morality. The first substage of principled morality, social contract or utility and individual rights, involves working for the greatest good for the greatest number. It comes about when people realize that the laws and norms of their society are not sacred but rather are rules created by the members of their society to facilitate social interaction. Such people realize that there is nothing sacred about driving on the right (left) side of the highway. People ride on the right (left) side of the highway simply to avoid collisions. When a rule no longer serves a useful function it should be changed. Cultural relativism is an important aspect of this stage of moral development. It is realized that different cultures have different rules because of their different environments and histories and that the rules of different cultures are equally valid. Individual relativism is also an aspect of this stage. It is realized that different people like different things and that these likes are equally valid. Because of the belief in both cultural and individual relativism, there is a great deal of emphasis on individual rights. Each person is encouraged to follow his or her preferences except when they interfere with the happiness of others. Social contract or utility and individual rights morality is the morality of the utilitarian philosophers, Bentham and Mills, and it was the official morality of the founding fathers of the United States. It is the morality that underlies the democratic system of government.

Universal Ethical Principles

The second substage of principled morality, universal ethical principles, demands behavior that is consistent with universal moral laws. These laws involve the principles of justice, that is, the equality of human rights and respect for the dignity of the individual. Social contract morality is a frustrating morality in that it does not point to any ultimate good beyond survival and noninterference. Morality of universal ethical principles goes beyond this kind of morality by pointing out that justice is the ultimate good. There exist universal moral laws that can be used to judge cultures and individuals. Persons functioning at this stage go along with the will of the majority and obey laws only when they are consistent with universal justice. When laws are not consistent with universal justice, they are disobeyed. Individuals who functioned at this stage include Socrates, Joan of Arc, Thoreau, and Martin Luther King, Jr.

In contrast to the theories of Maslow and Erikson, Kohlberg's theory of moral development has generated a great deal of research. One reason for this probably lies in the fact that tests of Kohlberg's stages of moral development have been created. Kohlberg (1958) has developed a projective measure of moral development, and more recently, James Rest and his associates have developed an objective measure (Rest, Cooper, Coder, Masanz, and Anderson, 1974). Kohlberg (1968) has found that moral development correlates positively with age for children living in the United States, Taiwan, Mexico, Turkey, and Malaya. Children living in the United States, however, progress through the stages more rapidly than children in the other cultures, suggesting that moral development may be a luxury. Furthermore, there is some evidence that the sequence of stages is invariant (Kohlberg, 1963; Rest, 1973; Rest, Turiel, and Kohlberg, 1969; Turiel, 1966). Other studies have found that moral development is positively correlated with intelligence and education (Rest et al., 1974) and guilt feelings, at least for Stages 1, 2, and 3 (Ruma and Mosher, 1967), and that it is negatively correlated with cheating (Schwartz, Feldman, Brown, and Heingartner, 1969) and delinquency (Fodor, 1972). Saltzstein,

Diamond, and Belenky (1972) found that Stage 3 individuals were most conforming, followed by Stage 1 and 2 individuals. Stage 4, 5, and 6 individuals were least conforming. Stanley Milgram (1963), in his famous studies of obedience, found that subjects at higher levels of moral development were less likely to obey an experimenter and give painful shocks to another subject than were subjects at lower levels of development. Finally, in an interesting study of social activism, Haan, Smith, and Block (1968) interviewed students at Berkeley to determine their level of moral development and whether or not they had participated in a free speech movement sit-in. They found the following percentages for males: 75 percent of the Stage 6 individuals participated, 41 percent of Stage 5, 6 percent of Stage 4, 18 percent of Stage 3, and 60 percent of Stage 2. It is interesting that although Stage 6 had the highest percentage of participants, it was closely followed by Stage 2. While this may seem to be evidence against Kohlberg's theory, I feel that it is, instead, a commentary on the activism of the 1960s. Many of the activists were motivated by lofty ideals, but others were only seeking excitement and sensual pleasure. Sara Davidson's (1977) biographical novel about the 1960s, *Loose Change,* substantiates this point.

A Synthesis of Maslow, Erikson, and Kohlberg

At this point I plan to show how the theories of Maslow, Erikson, and Kohlberg all point to a common sequence of value development. Each of these theorists seems to suggest that value development involves the expansion of concerns. At birth infants are concerned with only one thing, their immediate survival. As they mature physically and gain experience, they increase in competence so that their sphere of concerns expands to include long-range survival, the acquisition of an identity, involvement with other people, work, and (sometimes) the whole universe.

Maslow sees individuals as being initially concerned with immediate survival. Once their survival is secured, however, they expand the sphere of what they value to include long-range survival, that is, security. Once security has been acquired, they again expand their sphere of concern to include love, esteem, and, finally, self-actualization. In self-actualizing, people live in terms of metavalues, which are universal. In so doing, they are, in a sense, concerned with the whole universe.

Similarly, Erikson suggests that the first developmental task for newborn infants is to learn to survive in a new and possibly hostile world; they must establish a sense of trust. Once trust has been achieved, their sphere of concerns increases to include autonomy, initiative, and industry. During adolescence their value sphere further expands to include identity. After identity it expands to include other people and work (intimacy and generativity) and eventually, during the ego-integrity stage, the whole universe.

Finally, Kohlberg's preconventional morality takes into consideration a very limited sphere of concerns, an individual's own survival and happiness. As people develop, however, their morality expands to include not only themselves but also their immediate family, friends, and society. This occurs during the conventional level of moral development. The final level of moral development, postconventional morality, deals with an even greater sphere of concerns, which is the morality of the individual concerned with the entire universe.

The key to value development seems to lie in adequacy. As people become more capable, they become involved in more things, events, and people. They never give up a group of concerns to move on to others. Instead, they continue to add concerns to those they already have. For example, children do not give up their interest in survival when they become interested in security. Concern with security is added to their interest in survival. Similarly, young adults do not stop developing their own identities when they marry and have children. Their love for their spouses and children is added to their love for themselves.

It is interesting to note that value development moves from self-centeredness to altruism. This is in keeping with the prescriptions of the great religions of the world. Christians are taught to love their neighbors as themselves. Hindus believe that spiritual development involves realizing that the individual and God are one. Thus to harm another is to harm God and oneself, for all are one. And Buddhists aspire to become bodhisattvas, that is, compassionate beings who after earning nirvana chose not to enter it but rather return to their fellow human beings and help them to also achieve nirvana.

Although the expansion of the value sphere is a continual process like the expansion of a balloon being filled with air or the increasing area of a pond being filled with water, for the purpose of this book I am going to specify arbitrary areas. The smallest value sphere involves survival. Beyond survival are competence, self-enhancement, love and work, and, finally, the universe. This expanding value sphere is represented pictorially in Figure 1. In the remainder of the book I shall review the theory and data that are relevant to each of the value spheres.

Figure 1. Expanding Sphere of Values

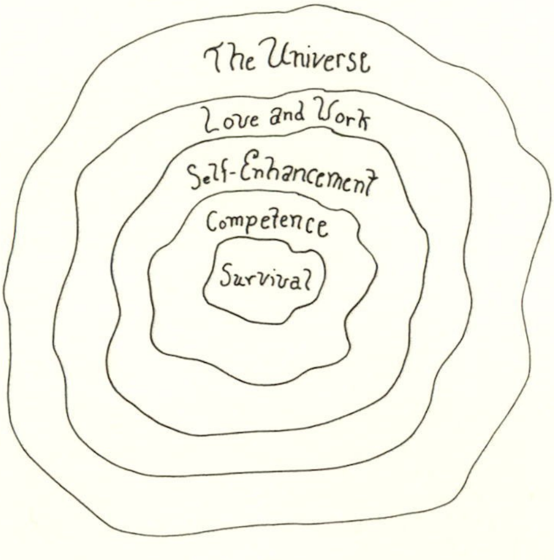

3. Survival

When a child is born, the first and most basic concern of that child is survival. This concern will continue until the moment of death. Maslow deals with survival when he discusses physiological needs. His most important point about physiological needs seems to be that they are prepotent to all other needs. Erikson deals with survival when he discusses his first developmental stage, trust. If newborn infants are to survive, they must come to the conclusion that the world is a satisfying place in which to live and that they are welcome. If children do not acquire a sense of trust, they will die. Kohlberg suggests that the morality of survival is heteronomous. Newborn infants are primarily concerned with avoiding punishments, that is, social events that might terminate their existence.

Prerequisite to All Else

The theory presented in the previous chapter suggests that survival is more basic than any other set of values. When a person's survival is threatened it is impossible for that person to care about anything else. Data from a study of semistarvation and prison camp experiences tend to confirm this. Keys, Brozek, Henschel, Mickelsen, and Taylor (1950, quoted in Coleman, 1956, p. 76) found that semistarvation produces the following results:

> During World War II, a study of semi-starvation was carried on at the University of Minnesota with 36 young conscientious objectors who volunteered for the experiment. Over the prolonged period of semi-starvation, dramatic personality changes were observed: constant preoccupation with thoughts of food and inability to concentrate on anything else; easy fatigability and preference for sedentary rather than active behavior; reduction and practical disappearance of sex drive coupled with a loss of interest in their girl friends; loss of sense of humor which was replaced by a feeling of depression and gloom; and a marked decrease in sociability together with irritability toward others. By the end of the 25th week, *the hunger drive had become the dominant influence in the behavior of the subjects*. Food dominated their thoughts, their conversations, their leisure-time activities, and their daydreams.

Viktor Frankl (1973), an Austrian psychiatrist who was incarcerated in a Nazi concentration camp during World War II, made similar observations concerning semistarvation. He found that sexual humor, talk, and activity entirely disappeared and that he and his fellow inmates spent most of their free time describing the lavish meals that they were going to serve each other when they got out of the camp.

Freud's Ideas about Survival

During the first half of this century, experimental psychologists believed that all values were rooted in physiological needs or derived from such needs through classical conditioning. As a result a large amount of research has been carried out on hunger, thirst, and sleep (see Cofer and Appley, 1964). However, since the satisfaction of these physiological needs tends to be automatic and nonproblematic for most individuals, I am not going to discuss these data. Instead I am going to deal with sex and aggression. In doing this I am following Sigmund Freud, who believed that sex and aggression, or eros and thanatos as he labeled them, are the most important of all the biological drives. Although neither sex nor aggression is absolutely necessary for the survival of the individual as are food, water, or sleep, they both play an extremely important role in survival when viewed from a broader perspective. Sex is necessary for the survival of species, and aggression is necessary for both the survival of predators and the animals on which they prey. Let us begin with sex.

The Problem of Sex

Freud felt that the human sex drive is a problem because it is extremely powerful and because it tends to clash with the rules of civilized cooperation. Human beings are saddled with powerful sex drives as a result of evolution. Species that evolved powerful sex drives produced numerous offspring and survived while species that did not evolve powerful sex drives have disappeared. Although reproduction is necessary for species survival, it is often detrimental to the survival of the individual. The pregnant female is vulnerable to predators, disease, and accidents, and birth often causes death to the mother. As Carl Rogers (1977) has commented, before modern medicine, men literally loved their women to death. To overcome the woman's reluctance to subject herself to these dangers, the sex drive has had to become powerful, obsessive, and extremely pleasurable.

The Power of the Sex Drive and Irrational Behavior

Because the sex drive is so powerful it often causes the individual to engage in irrational and dangerous behavior. This point is well illustrated by the sexual behavior of the praying mantis. Once the male and female have embraced each other and are connected in sexual intercourse, the female bites off the male's head. The male's death convulsions complete the copulation. The female then lays her fertilized eggs in the body of the male so that the offspring will have something to eat when they are born. If male mantises were not so strongly motivated sexually, they would live longer although the species would probably disappear.

Not only praying mantises but also human beings fall prey to powerful sexual drives. Victor Hugo's novel, *The Hunchback of Notre Dame,* captures the irrationality of human sexuality extremely well. In this novel, a priest is distracted by music while praying in one of the towers of Notre Dame Cathedral. To eliminate the distraction he gets up to close his window. Before closing the window, however, he looks out to discover the source of the music. Below him he sees a beautiful gypsy girl playing a tambourine and dancing for coins. He instantly falls in love with her. After closing the window and returning to his prayers, he cannot get her out of his mind. He feels guilty because priests are not supposed to appreciate the flesh. Thereafter he is compelled to follow her about Paris lusting after her and hating her. Finally because he cannot endure his misery any longer, he has her arrested for witchcraft. (The accusation is based on the fact that in her act she dances with a trained goat.) During her trial she is threatened with torture, and therefore she confesses and is sentenced to hang the next day. That night the priest slips into her dungeon cell and explains to her that he is responsible for her plight because he loves her so much. He then offers to save her life if she will marry him and live with him in southern Greece. She refuses because she is in love with a young soldier; therefore, the next day she is hanged.

A subplot of the novel deals with the priest's adopted son who is an ugly hunchback. He, too, falls in love with the beautiful gypsy girl. To revenge her death he kills his father by pushing him out of one of the cathedral windows. He then seeks out the girl's body, which has been thrown into a garbage pit outside Paris, and lovingly holds her in his arms until he dies of starvation.

Unfortunately, fiction does not constitute the best scientific data. To rectify this situation, I shall present empirical data. In a questionnaire study, Eugene Kanin (1967) found that approximately 25 percent of the men attending a midwestern university admitted that in attempting sexual intercourse they had used force to the point where the woman fought, cried, screamed, or pleaded that they stop. I know of no other social activity in which this kind of pressure is used.

Recently, social psychologists have discovered that an individual's physical attractiveness is extremely important in determining success with people of the opposite sex. It has been found that men give attractive women more love (Mathes, 1975; Walsten, Aronson, Abrahams, and Rottmann, 1966), empathy (Barocas and Karoly, 1971), money (Mathes and Edwards, 1978b), marriage proposals (Holmes and Hatch, 1936), social status through marriage (Elder, 1969), sexual gratification (Kaats and Davis, 1970), work (Sigall, Page, and Brown, 1971), and compliance (Mills and Aronson, 1965) than they give unattractive women. Other research suggests that women also give good outcomes to attractive men (Mathes and Edwards, 1978b). These results cannot be accounted for by aesthetics since attractiveness gains nothing from individuals of the same sex. These data, therefore, have to be explained by human sexuality. It is believed that attractive people are more desirable sex objects and thus it is agreed that they "deserve" good outcomes. But do they really deserve these advantages? Should not all social rewards be earned through constructive activity?

Sex in Conflict with Civilization

Freud's second reason for feeling that sex is a problem is that it tends to conflict with social rules. Freud (1961b) observed that when human beings were still asocial creatures, they developed powerful and promiscuous sex drives. Numerous copulations meant numerous offspring and species success. With time, however, the family and other forms of civilized cooperation developed that resulted in raising the odds of species survival even more. This evolutionary development, however, has placed human beings in a difficult situation. Cooperative living requires that sexual activity be limited to appropriate times, places, and partners. Human sexuality thus clashes with civilization. Secretly, all human begins would like to throw off their clothes and fornicate with dozens of different partners. At the same time, they realize that such activity would have disastrous effects on society. Unwanted children would abound, work would cease, social diseases would be rampant, and jealousy would be widespread. They are caught in a bind. Sexual control produces frustration while sexual freedom produces anarchy.

Freud felt that this conflict between *Homo sapiens'* earlier "animal" nature and recently acquired civilization is the root of all neuroses. Furthermore, he felt that this conflict could not be resolved; thus, he was pessimistic about human happiness. He believed that the best one can do is to be aware of one's fate and stoically endure it. Psychoanalysis does not attempt to resolve this conflict. It simply helps the individual to face it instead of running away from it.

Easing the Sex versus Civilization Conflict–Freud and Technology

Although it may never be possible to totally eliminate the conflict between human sexuality and civilization, I feel that there are various things that can be done to partially alleviate it. Freud did a great deal himself simply by pointing out the dilemma so that people could deal with it more intelligently. Because of Freud, the extreme sexual repression of the Victorian era has eased. Technology has also been helpful. Venereal diseases can be effectively treated with penicillin and other antibiotics, and the birth control pill has made it possible to avoid unwanted pregnancies.

Technology has eliminated many of the aversive social consequences of nonmonogamous sexual activity. Taking advantage of the separation of sex and reproduction, which birth control allows, young people have been engaging in continuously increasing premarital sexual activity. Thus, by 1980 premarital sex should be almost universal (Hunt, 1974). The taboos against extramarital sex are also being weakened, as is evidenced by the popularity of books like the O'Neills (1973) *Open Marriage* and the phenomenon of mate swapping. M. Hunt, who has extensively researched the sexual trends of the 1970s, however, suggests that extramarital sex will not become as widespread as premarital sex owing to the problem of jealousy. Even individuals who do not want to be sexually possessive of their mates, such as swinging couples, seem to have problems with jealousy (Gilmartin, 1977).

Easing the Sex versus Civilization Conflict–Research

Greater permissiveness about sex has not only led to an increase in quantity of sexual activity but, probably, also quality. Sex education has been introduced into some public schools. Many books on sexual technique and sensuality have been published. In addition, empirical research on human sexuality has begun. Alfred Kinsey and his associates (Kinsey, Pomeroy, and Martin, 1948; Kinsey, Pomeroy, Martin, and Gebhard, 1953) pioneered this research with their investigations of the extent of various kinds of sexual activity among Americans. More recently, William Masters and Virginia Johnson (1966, 1970) have studied in detail the physiology of the human sexual response. They have also developed effective therapies for dealing with various sexual dysfunctions. The research of Masters and Johnson has cleared up a variety of sexual myths, such as the vaginal orgasm, and has helped people to enjoy their sexuality to a much greater extent than before.

One important area of research is sex differences in sexuality. Do men enjoy sex more than women? Since women can copulate and even conceive children without having sexual orgasms or enjoying sex, women do not necessarily have to have a sex drive to keep the species reproducing. This is not true for men. Thus it may follow that women do not have sex drives as powerful as those of men.

Do the data support this conclusion? Different studies provide different answers. Kinsey and others (1953) found that a much higher proportion of males than females reported that they enjoyed erotic materials such as pictures of nudes. Although it may be speculated that these results were found because the double standard was in force in the 1950s, a later nationwide survey produced similar results (Abelson, Cohen, Heaton, and Suder, 1971). In contrast to these studies, a study carried out by Donn Byrne and J. Lamberth (1971), in which married couples were exposed to erotic pictures, literature, and imagery, found that men and women reported equal arousal. Finally, a study by B. Kutschinsky (1971), in which men and women in Copenhagen were exposed to one hour of hard-core pornography, found that men "heated up" more quickly than women but also "cooled off" more rapidly with the result that at the end of the hour there was no difference in arousal. At this point a definitive answer to the question of sex differences cannot be given. It may be that this question can never be answered because a common ground of comparison cannot be found. It is impossible for a man to experience the sexuality of a woman or vice versa.

Is Sex Best in Moderation?

Although there is a great deal of descriptive research about the frequency and mechanics of human sexual behavior, little research exists on how it can be most effectively handled. Although the repressive attitude of the Victorian era was undoubtedly unhealthy, it is not clear that total permissiveness is a better alternative. Being forced to compete with others in terms of number of partners, lasting power, expertise, and orgasms can be as oppressive as being forced to abstain (May, 1973). Furthermore, giving in to a powerful force is not intrinsically more rational than total resistance. A middle-way approach to sexuality in which there is neither celibacy nor total promiscuity would seem most appropriate. I do not think that Freud would quarrel with this conclusion. Unfortunately, I have no research to support (or deny) this strategy.

The Problem of Aggression

Late in his career, Freud (1961a) revamped his theory of personality to suggest that sex has a powerful twin in aggression. In other words, people are driven not only to engage in sex but also aggression. He called these two forces eros, the life instinct, and thanatos, the death instinct. During youth, the death instinct is primarily oriented against others. As people grow older, however, their death instinct turns more and more on themselves, and they age. In the end, thanatos wins over eros, and people die. According to Freud, the goal of life is death. World War I was partially responsible for the revision of Freud's theory. If making love represents the meaning of life, why was all the world making war? To answer this question, Freud postulated a death instinct. It has also been suggested that Freud's own aging and his cancer of the jaw were partially responsible for the revision (Schultz, 1976).

Life and Death as Intricate Parts of Nature

Is there support for Freud's theory of aggression? On the cosmic level, at least, it seems to make sense. Throughout the universe, creation and destruction seem to go on constantly. Plants come up in the spring and then wither away and die in the fall. A child is born, grows to maturity, then ages and dies. The Rocky Mountains are being thrust upward and the Appalachians are being worn away. The Hindus represent this process by the dance of Shiva, which involves both creation and destruction. Taoists see nature as involving both the yin and the yang. Since human beings are a part of the universe, the forces of creation and destruction should also be found in them.

Aggression and Survival

Aggression seems to be at least as important as sex for species survival. For predators, a strong tendency toward aggression insures that they will eat. Strong tendencies by those preyed upon help them to avoid being eaten. Not only is interspecies aggression adaptive, but intraspecies aggression also has survival value. Intraspecies aggression insures that the strongest and most fit males will father the next generation. Burney LeBoeuf (1974) found that among elephant seals the dominant male in a group of 185 females and 120 males was responsible for approximately half of the observed copulations, and Sherwood Washburn and David Hamburg (1965) observed that the dominant male in a monkey colony also dominated reproduction.

Is Aggression a Drive?

Is aggression a drive like sex? That is, do people engage in aggression for pleasure and as an end in itself, or is it only used for instrumental and defensive purposes? To some extent, it probably is a drive. How else is one to explain the activities of the Hell's Angels and punk rockers, and the sports of football, boxing, and bullfighting? Sadie, a member of Charlie Manson's family, described the killing of Sharon Tate as follows: "It felt so good, the first time I stabbed her" (Sanders, 1972, p. 285). And everyone has probably experienced the pleasure of squashing bugs, popping balloons, and teasing younger siblings.

Little research has been carried out on this conception of aggression. This is probably because most of us would like to ignore the fact that we are capable of enjoying "senseless destruction." P. Zimbardo (1969) and I (Mathes and Guest, 1976; Mathes and Kahn, 1975), however, have independently carried out research that demonstrates that deindividuation, that is, losing one's individuality through disguises or being part of a mob, releases aggressive and destructive tendencies. With respect to individual differences, it has been found that men are five times more likely to kill than women (Edmiston, 1970) and that men having an extra Y chromosome ("supermen") tend to be especially prone to violence (Telfer, Baker, Clark, and Richardson, 1968).

Most of the research on the drive theory of aggression has centered on the notion of catharsis. Freud suggested that the aggression drive does not have to be satisfied through actual aggression. It can be satisfied through fantasy or through viewing the aggression of others. He labeled the latter process "catharsis." Seymour Feshback (1955) has found some support for the concept of catharsis. Insulted students who were allowed to write imaginative stories involving aggression engaged in less direct aggression when given the opportunity than a control group who had not written stories. Unfortunately, J. E. Hokanson and S. Shelter (1961) were unable to replicate this result.

Studies that have looked at the effects of viewing aggression have found that, contrary to the catharsis theory, viewing aggression generally increases aggressive behavior (see Liebert and Baron, 1972). Only when the viewed aggression is so brutal that it results in serious injury or death does viewing violence decrease subsequent aggressive behavior (Goranson, 1969). This effect, however, is probably not due to catharsis but rather the anxiety produced by the brutal effects of the aggression. A study by Eron, Lefkowitz, Huesmann, and Walder (1972) has even shown that the amount of television violence watched by nine-year-old boys was predictive of how aggressive the boys were ten years later at age nineteen. Thus, contrary to the wishes of network executives, the catharsis hypothesis does not seem to be true. Although watching violence sells breakfast cereal, it does not reduce aggressive behavior. On the contrary, it increases it. The failure of the catharsis hypothesis, however, does not necessarily invalidate the aggression drive theory.

Instrumental and Provoked Aggression

Most of the research on aggression has looked at instrumental and provoked aggression. That aggression can be instrumental, that is, used to obtain various goals, is quite obvious. Many parents use aggression in the form of punishment to socialize their children. The United States government spends more money on the military establishment than anything else. Organized crime has learned how to use aggression effectively, and our entire system of law enforcement is based on punishment. Research on instrumental aggression suggests that its effectiveness, however, is limited. Sears, Maccoby, and Levin (1957) found that parents who severely punished aggressive behavior by their children increased the aggression rather than decreased it. B. F. Skinner suggests that punishment and threat of punishment do not decrease antisocial behavior. Instead, people learn how to avoid punishment and still engage in antisocial behavior. Thus, when the speed limit was lowered to 55 miles per hour people did not slow down. Instead they bought CB radios and radar detectors so that they could break the law and not get caught. Finally, the data tend to suggest that capital punishment does not prevent murder (Clinard, 1963).

Research on provoked aggression has shown that frustration and attack are the two most reliable causes of this kind of aggression. One of the earliest tests of the frustration-produces-aggression hypothesis was carried out by Roger Barker, Tamara Dembo, and Kurt Lewin (1941). In their experiment they led little children to believe that they were going to get to play with attractive new toys and then prevented them from doing this with a wire screen. When they finally allowed the children to play with the toys, they were much more destructive towards the toys than a group of children who had not been frustrated. The hypothesis that attack produces aggression has been dramatically demonstrated by R. E. Ulrich (1966; Ulrich and Azrin, 1962). He found that when one rat is placed in a cage and given an electric shock it will attempt to escape the situation. However, when two rats are placed in a cage and shocked, they attack each other. S. P. Taylor and his colleagues (Gaebelein and Taylor, 1971; Taylor, 1967, 1970; Taylor and Epstein, 1967) have found empirical support for the attack-produces-aggression hypothesis with human subjects. In their experiments, they led pairs of subjects to believe that they were participating in a reaction time game in which the faster subject was allowed to select a shock intensity for the slower subject to receive. It was found that subjects receiving powerful shocks from an opponent tended to pay back the opponent in kind when given an opportunity.

Aggression versus Civilization

Freud (1961a) suggests that aggression is a problem for humanity for the same reason that sex is a problem. When human beings were still asocial creatures they evolved powerful aggressive tendencies because aggression facilitated survival. Since then, however, we have discovered that civilized cooperation is even more effective in facilitating survival than aggression. As a result we find ourselves in the position of having powerful aggressive tendencies that must be kept in check it we are to live peacefully with each other. As with the conflict of sex versus civilization, Freud felt that the conflict of aggression versus civilization could not be resolved. Again, however, Freud may have been overly pessimistic.

Ways of Solving the Problem of Aggression

Aggression for pleasure seems to be a rare phenomenon and hence is not too much of a problem. It certainly is more rare than sex for pleasure. Instrumental aggression and provoked aggression seem to constitute a much greater problem. On the interpersonal level, Alberti and Emmons (1974) suggest that instrumental aggression can be effectively eliminated through assertiveness training. They suggest that people engage in instrumental aggression because they have not learned more effective ways of satisfying their needs. Teaching such individuals assertiveness eliminates their need to use instrumental aggression. On the international level, the prospect is more bleak. At any moment the third and last world war may begin. The only hope that I can see for this situation lies in developing a world organization through which all nations can work for the common good of humanity. This plan is based on M. Sherif's (1967) superordinate goal theory and research. Sherif found that conflicting parties could be brought together if they became involved in the attainment of a goal that both wanted but neither could obtain alone. Maybe all of the peoples of the world could work together to eliminate disease, hunger, pollution, waste, and overpopulation. In this manner war would be eliminated.

For provoked aggression, it has been found that frustration and attack do not always lead to aggression. The intentions of the person producing the frustration or attack are important. In general, only frustration or attack that has been intentional is responded to with counteraggression. Although everyone has probably experienced pain at the hands of the dentist, such "attacks" usually did not result in aggression since the intentions of the dentist were constructive. An experiment supporting this point was carried out by J. Greenwell and H. A. Dengerink (1971). These researchers used a variation of the reaction time game in which subjects were first given information about the intensity of the shock their opponent intended to give them and then were given the shock. The experimenters rigged the game so that some of the subjects received information that stated that their opponent's intended shock was increasing over trials while the shock was actually maintained at a moderate level. Other subjects received information that their opponent's intended shock was being maintained at a constant moderate level over trials while the shock was actually being increased over trials. It was found that in counterattacks, subjects responded to the information about the opponent's intention and not the actual shock. Thus subjects in the first condition gave increasingly severe shocks to their opponents, and subjects in the second condition maintained a constant level of countershock.

It has also been shown that the anger produced by frustration or attack can be reduced by events other than counteraggression. For example, Baron (1972; Baron and Ball, 1974) has found that pleasurable activities such as humor or looking at *Playboy* centerfolds eliminate the anger produced by attack. Hokanson and his associates (Hokanson, 1970; Hokanson and Burgess, 1962; Hokanson, Burgess, and Cohen, 1963; Hokanson and Edelman, 1966; Hokanson and Shelter, 1963; Hokanson, Willers, and Koropsak, 1968) have shown that while the physiological indices of anger, increased systolic blood pressure and heart rate, can be reduced by physical or verbal counterattack, these physiological indices can also be reduced in other ways. For women and passive men (Sosa, 1968) a friendly response to their attacker was found to reduce blood pressure and heart rate. Stone and Hokanson (1969) have even found that subjects who responded to attack with self-aggression (self-shock) reduced the physiological correlates of anger.

How to Handle Anger

Taking this research into consideration, clinical psychologists (Alberti and Emmons, 1974; Bach and Goldberg, 1975) have suggested several ways of dealing with the anger that inevitably arises within close interpersonal relationships. (As the popular song goes, "You always hurt the one you love.") Clinical psychologists suggest that when anger does arise it is best for the angered individual to face this anger and bring it to the attention of the frustrating or attacking individual. In bringing anger to the attention of the other person, it is important that this be accomplished without accusation or counterattack. This is to prevent the other person from becoming angry. Attack followed by counterattack will result in further attack and never-ending escalation. For example, it is better to say, "When you didn't pick me up for the junior prom I felt rejected and angry," than to say, "You no good, lowdown, miserable bastard! Why weren't you here to take me to the junior prom? I'm so mad I could kill you." When the events leading to the anger are discussed, it will often be found that the frustration or attack was accidental, and the anger will then disappear. If, however, it is found that the frustration or attack was intentional, the result of a real conflict of interests, it is important that the individuals work out a compromise to minimize and share the hurt. The care shown in this act of compromise will do much to relieve the offended individual's anger. If the partner refuses to cooperate in working out a solution, it is probably best to discontinue the relationship. Although it has been shown that masochism does reduce anger, in the long run masochism is maladaptive both to the masochist and the tormentor. Repeated masochistic acts produce hatred for the tormentor (Fromm, 1941). If this pent-up hatred does not lead to the demise of the tormentor, the tormentor will become bored with the masochist and probably leave the relationship voluntarily.

Is Death Caused by the Death Instinct?

What about Freud's hypothesis that aging and death are caused by the turning of thanatos onto the individual? Are not aging and death simply the products of disease and a worn-out organism? The data suggest that aging and death are not simply the products of disease and wear and tear. Instead, they are to some extent genetically determined. At birth the individual has already been programmed to grow old and die. Each species has an upper age limit beyond which individuals do not live (Kurtzman and Gordon, 1977). Furthermore, F. A. Kallman and G. Sanders (1948) have shown that each individual's aging and death are genetically controlled. In studying identical twins (twins with identical genetic makeups), they found that when one twin dies of old age the other will die within an average of 36.9 months.

For evolution, species survival is facilitated by individual death. Maintaining a given model of a complex organism and simply reproducing enough copies to replace those eliminated by accidents does not provide the flexibility necessary for species survival in an ever-changing environment. This flexibility is obtained by periodically scrapping old models through death and beginning anew with a different set of organisms resulting from mutation and sexual reproduction.

Thus it appears that Freud was right to some extent. Aging and death come from within, not without. I know of no data, however, that suggest that individuals pursue aging and death like they pursue sex; most individuals find aging and death highly aversive. Elizabeth Kübler-Ross (1970), in interviewing terminally ill patients, has found that they resist death almost to the end. When terminally ill patients are initially informed of their impending death, they respond with denial. They claim that a mistake has been made—the x-rays have been mixed up, for example. As patients become weaker and denial is no longer possible, they respond with anger followed by bargaining for a little more time. When this tactic fails, depression sets in. If patients live long enough to work through their anger, bargaining, and depression, they finally reach a point where they quietly accept their death. Although many terminally ill patients come to accept death, acceptance seems to be embraced only because there is no alternative. Thus Freud's belief that there is a self-destruction drive that functions like the sex drive seems to be erroneous.

Is It Possible to Die Happily?

What is necessary for a happy death? Death is not difficult to accomplish like obtaining a college degree or finding a good woman to marry. It is easy. Everyone sooner or later succeeds in dying. What makes dying aversive and traumatic is the intense desire of most people to live. After having invested so much in living, death seems like a cruel trick. Why spend so much time, effort, and resources fighting death since death wins in the end, anyhow? Why not give up immediately after birth? It is not surprising that the fact of death has made many people cynical about life. Blaise Pascal called life a "terminal illness." And Albert Camus (1955) likened life to Sisyphus's fate of having to roll a stone up a mountain only to have it roll down, causing Sisyphus to have to start all over again.

The Christian View of Life after Death

But not everyone is so negative toward death. The attitude taken toward death is to a large extent determined by the individual's beliefs about what happens after death. For centuries the Western World has followed the Christian view of death. It has believed that after death the individual either goes to heaven or hell depending upon whether or not the individual had accepted God's grace while on earth. Therefore, death for the believer was not a traumatic event. Kübler-Ross (1970), however, suggests that today the Christian belief system does not have the power that it once had and that people seem to have no firm idea of what follows death.

Materialism and Death

Another answer to the question of life after death that is popular, at least among materialists, is that death is simply the end. When the body ceases to function, consciousness ends, and the remains are eaten by worms and eventually turn to dust. Life after death exists only insofar as the remains of the body are incorporated into some other form of life, for example, a worm or flower (Watts, 1973). This is the answer given by Freud. It has also been indirectly supported by early experimental psychology, that is, behaviorism. Behaviorists believed that the body and behavior are all that are real and worthy of scientific investigation. Consciousness was seen as either a myth like ghosts and spirits, or a quaint, useless phenomenon that simply tagged along after physiology and behavior. Thus, when the body died, consciousness ceased and life was finished. Persons who believe that existence ceases at death are working to discover ways of altering the genetic code so that aging and death will not occur. Some scientists believe that this will be accomplished by the year 2000 (Kurtzman and Gordon, 1977).

Consciousness May Continue after Death

Recently, however, psychologists have become interested again in consciousness (see Ornstein, 1972; Tart, 1975). Consciousness is now seen as functional, and empirical investigations of it are being carried out. Some psychologists, particularly those interested in parapsychological phenomena, feel that it has an existence independent of the body. As a result, psychologists are becoming more open to the possibility that consciousness may continue after death. Data supporting this hypothesis come from Raymond Moody's (1976) interviews with clinically dead individuals who have been resuscitated, Ian Stevenson's (1974) carefully documented cases of reincarnation, and reports of contacting the dead through mediums. Let us examine these data.

In interviewing clinically dead individuals who had been resuscitated, Moody (1975) found that many of these individuals had not lost consciousness upon "dying." Instead, all had similar experiences that included the following features (Moody, 1975, pp. 21–23):

A man is dying and, as he reaches the point of greatest physical distress, he hears himself pronounced dead by his doctor. He begins to hear an uncomfortable noise, a loud ringing or buzzing, and at the same time he feels himself moving very rapidly through a long dark tunnel. After this, he suddenly finds himself outside of his own physical body, but still in the immediate physical environment, and he sees his own body from a distance, as though he is a spectator. He watches the resuscitation attempt from this unusual vantage point and is in a state of emotional upheaval.

After a while, he collects himself and becomes more accustomed to his odd condition. He notices that he still has a "body," but one of a very different nature and with very different powers from the physical body he has left behind. Soon other things begin to happen. Others come to meet and to help him. He glimpses the spirits of relatives and friends who have already died, and a loving, warm spirit of a kind he has never encountered before—a being of light—appears before him. This being asks him a question, nonverbally, to make him evaluate his life and helps him along by showing him a panoramic, instantaneous playback of the major events of his life. At some point he finds himself approaching some sort of barrier or border, apparently representing the limit between earthly life and the next life. Yet, he finds that he must go back to the earth, that the time for his death has not yet come. At this point he resists, for by now he is taken up with his experiences in the afterlife and does not want to return. He is overwhelmed by intense feelings of joy, love, and peace. Despite his attitude, though, he somehow reunites with his physical body and lives.

Later he tries to tell others, but he has trouble doing so. In the first place, he can find no human words adequate to describe these unearthly episodes. He also finds that others scoff, so he stops telling other people. Still, the experience affects his life profoundly, especially his views about death and its relationship to life.

Whether or not an individual's awareness continues indefinitely after the death of the body cannot be determined by these data. The experiences of these people may simply have been hallucinations. The fact, however, that these experiences are so similar argues against the hallucination hypothesis. If these hallucinations are like those caused by LSD, some people should experience heaven, others hell, and atheists should experience nothing at all. This, however, does not happen. All of the experiences are similar regardless of the individual's conception of the afterlife. On the other hand, if two people stare at a neon sign and then close their eyes, the afterimages (hallucinations) experienced by the two people will also be highly similar. Possibly there is something about the physiology of death that produces identical hallucinations for different people. More research is necessary to answer these questions.

Ian Stevenson (1974) has investigated a number of cases of reincarnation in which young children have reported memories of a previous life, memories which were subsequently validated. The case of Prakash is typical.

In April 1950, Nirmal Jain died of smallpox at his parents' home in Kosi Kalan. Before he died, however, he twice said to his mother that she was not his mother, that she was a Jatni, and that he was going to his real mother. While saying this he pointed in the direction of the town of Chhatta. In August 1951 a son was born to Sri Brijlal Varshnay of Chhatta, and he was named Prakash. At about age four and a half he began waking in the middle of the night and running out into the street explaining that his name was Nirmal and that he wanted to go to his old home in Kosi Kalan. To quiet him, in 1956 his uncle agreed to take him to Kosi Kalan. When his uncle boarded the bus going away from Kosi Kalan, Prakash pointed out the error, and they then boarded the correct bus. Upon arriving at Kosi Kalan he led his uncle to Sri Bholanath Jain's shop but did not recognize it, possibly because it was closed. (Sri Bholanath Jain had moved to Delhi.)

In the spring of 1961, after his return to Kosi Kalan, Sri Bholanath Jain heard about Prakash and decided to visit him with his daughter Memo. Upon meeting, Prakash recognized his "father" and partially recognized Memo, mistaking her for another sister. Later, Nirmal's mother, older sister, and brother visited Prakash, and he wept with joy upon seeing his older sister. The Jain family then persuaded the parents of Prakash to allow him to visit Kosi Kalan again. Upon arrival Prakash again led the way to the Jain home and, once there, recognized Nirmal's other brother, two aunts, some neighbors, and parts of the house.

In July 1961 Stevenson visited Prakash with Sri Jagdish Jain, whom Prakash recognized, and interviewed both Prakash and his family. He again visited the Varshnay family in 1964 to obtain more information.

Stevenson's careful documentation makes it very difficult to resist the conclusion that at least some individuals are reincarnated.

Although the notion of reincarnation may seem attractive to Westerners who believe in the "worms and dust" theory, discovering that it may very well be true seems to take some attractiveness away. Having to start life over and over again and relearn how to walk, talk, pass kindergarten, get a job, and relate to men or women seems a bit depressing. Such thoughts cause an appreciation for the desire of Hindus and Buddhists for moksha, or release from repeated reincarnations. Ironically, Hindus and Buddhists believe that they must work for the cessation of consciousness, whereas many Westerners believe that it is the automatic result of death and something to be dreaded.

A final source of evidence suggesting that consciousness continues after death is the large number of reports of having contacted the dead through mediums. Bishop Pike's (1969) account of his contacts with his teenage son who committed suicide is an example of this kind of data. Unfortunately, no one has studied this phenomenon as carefully as Moody has studied cases of resuscitated clinical death or Stevenson has studied cases of reincarnation.

With these data in mind it is again possible to ask what is necessary for a happy death. In a statistical study that involved interviewing terminally ill patients, Raymond Carey (1975) found that pain more than any other factor created a poor emotional adjustment by the dying person. Factors that facilitated adjustment included previous contact with a person who was dying and accepted death with inner peace, an intrinsic religion (though Christians, in general, were more adjusted than non-Christians), support from family and friends, and education. As a result of her extensive work with the terminally ill, Kübler-Ross suggests that the greatest defense against a miserable death is having lived a full life. Erik Erikson (1963) echoes this point, suggesting that the individual who has successfully completed all of the stages of development accepts death with dignity. Those who have not completed all of the stages face death with despair. Regardless of whether death is final, heralds reincarnation, or leads to some kind of nonmaterial existence, living the present life fully would seem to make death least aversive.

4. Competence

Once people have worked out ways of insuring their immediate physiological survival and have time, energy, and resources to spare, the value sphere expands to include competence. The acquisition of competencies insures that people will survive not only today but also tomorrow, six months from now, and even in the distant future.

The Importance of Competence

Competence differs from survival in that survival is centered in the present whereas competence takes into consideration not only the present but also the future. Competence involves both the acquisition of skills like walking, talking, reading, and playing tennis and the acquisition of beliefs such as the notions that the world is orderly and that one is a capable individual. Maslow (1939; 1940; 1942) deals with competence when he discusses security. He first became interested in security as a result of his studies of dominance in monkeys. Later he developed a scale, which he called the Security-Insecurity Scale, for measuring security in human beings. Linda Edwards and I (Mathes and Edwards, 1978) have used this scale to test Maslow's hypothesis that security is a prerequisite for self-actualization and have found support for it. Erikson deals most directly with competence in his discussion of the autonomy, initiative, and industry stages of development, though all of his stages deal with skill acquisition. The morality of competence is Kohlberg's instrumental purpose and exchange, his second stage of moral development.

As noted earlier, during the first half of the present century experimental psychologists believed that all values were rooted in physiological needs or derived from them through classical conditioning. It was believed that the preferred state of animals and people was sleep. Organisms woke up and moved about only when they were driven to it by hunger, thirst, or sexual needs. Only in the 1950s was it discovered that satiated animals remained active. Harry Harlow found that monkeys would learn to solve mechanical puzzles without being rewarded (Harlow, Harlow, and Myers, 1950), and R. A. Butler (1953) found that monkeys would solve problems for the privilege of peeking out of an opaque cage into the laboratory. It was concluded that animals and people live for more than bread. Competence is one of the additional factors for which organisms live.

A great deal of work has been done on competence. General intelligence, an important aspect of competence, has been thoroughly researched. The neo-Freudians, Erik Erikson, Erich Fromm, and Karen Horney, have emphasized the importance of competence, using the term "ego-strength" for psychological health. The psychologists of individual differences, Frank Barron and Julian Rotter, have devised scales to measure competence, the Ego Strength Scale, and the Internal-External Locus of Control Scale. The experimental psychologists, Martin Seligman and C. P. Richter, have studied competence by making animals helpless; they have found that helplessness (that is, incompetence) has dire effects, including anxiety, depression, and death. Social and personality psychologists have studied competence in terms of ability to resist external pressure and need for achievement. Finally, clinical psychologists have developed a number of therapies to build competence, including various behavior therapies, assertiveness training, Albert Ellis's rational-emotive therapy, and William Glasser's reality therapy. In this chapter I am going to review each of these areas of research.

Intelligence and Competence

Competence is to some extent determined by intelligence. The more intelligent an individual is the more successful that person will be in dealing with the environment. Alfred Binet was the first person to develop a successful measure of intelligence (Byrne, 1974). In 1904 he was asked to develop a test for the school children in Paris to identify "feebleminded" children so that they could be placed in special schools. An objective measure of intelligence was needed to keep teachers from dumping troublemakers in the special school while keeping "nice" children who really belonged in the special school in the regular classroom. In 1905 Binet and his colleague, Th. Simon, created the first intelligence test. It was composed of a series of tasks involving memory, comprehension, and mathematical manipulation that varied in difficulty. The tasks were ordered from least to most difficult, and a child's intelligence was viewed as proportional to the number of tasks the child could complete.

In 1916 Lewis M. Terman developed an intelligence test, which he called the Stanford Binet, for use in the United States (Byrne, 1974). This test was composed of ninety items of the type used by Binet. The items that were included in the Stanford Binet were selected because they discriminated between children of different ages (that is, younger children were less likely to pass them than older children) and because they correlated with total test scores. During World War I Terman devised the first group intelligence test for the armed forces. (The Stanford Binet was such that it could be given to only one person at a time.) Since then many other intelligence tests have been devised, the most famous of which have been revisions of the Stanford Binet and the Wechsler Adult Intelligence Scale (WAIS).

Heredity and Intelligence

Which is more important in determining intelligence, genetic or environmental factors? Twin studies and studies of adopted children suggest that genetic factors are extremely important in determining intelligence. Gottesman (1963) has found that the intelligences of fraternal twins, that is, twins who do not have identical genetic makeup, only correlate about .60, while the intelligences of identical twins (twins with identical genetic makeups) correlate in the .80s. If intelligence were entirely determined by environmental experiences, these two correlations should be equal because twins, whether they are fraternal or identical, are typically raised in highly similar environments. In a study of children who were adopted before the age of six months, Skodak and Skeels (1949) found that at age thirteen the children's intelligences correlate about .40 with the intelligence of their biological parents and about .00, that is, not at all, with the intelligence of their adopted parents. Thirteen years of living with their adopted parents had no effect whatsoever on their intelligence.

Environment and Intelligence

On the other hand, studies of maternal nutrition and deprived and enriched environments suggest that environment is also extremely important in determining intelligence. To study the effects of prenatal maternal nutrition on the intelligence of children, Harrell, Woodyard, and Gates (1955) divided mothers attending a large maternity clinic in Norfolk, Virginia, into four groups. Each group of mothers was given a different kind of pill to take: a placebo (pills containing no nutrient material), ascorbic acid, thiamine, or a multinutrient pill composed of thiamine, riboflavin, niacinamide, and iron. The pills were taken during pregnancy and nursing. At age four the IQs of the children were tested with the resulting mean scores: placebo, 93.7; thiamine, 97.6; ascorbic acid, 97.9; and multinutrient, 101.6. The mother's nutrition had a definite effect on her child's intelligence.

Being raised in a nonstimulating environment has been found to have detrimental effects on intelligence. Gordon (1923) found that the average IQ of English canal-boat children was only 69.6. Canal-boat children attended school infrequently, and their parents were typically illiterate. Goldfarb (1945) found that children who were adopted in infancy had higher IQs than children who spent the first three years of their lives in an institution before being adopted. The average IQ of the initial group was 96, while that of the latter was only 68.

Enriched environments increase intelligence. Kirk (1958) has found evidence that attending nursery school increases IQ, and Don C. Charles and S. A. Pritchard (1959) found that attending college adds about twenty points to an individual's IQ.

Both Heredity and Environment Are Important

The controversy about whether heredity or environment is more important in determining intelligence raged during the first half of this century until it was realized that a definitive answer to this question could never be given. Both heredity and environment are important in determining intelligence. For mongoloid children who have been raised in normal environments, genetic factors are more important than environmental factors. (Mongoloidism is a form of mental retardation that has been found to be produced by chromosome abnormalities.) For individuals who have been raised under conditions of severe deprivation (for example, illegitimate children locked away in attics), environment is more important than heredity. For most people, however, heredity and environment are about equally important.

Are Geniuses Morbid Losers?

If you had the choice of a below-average IQ of 60, an average IQ of 100, or an above-average IQ of 140, which would you choose? If you did not choose the IQ of 140, was it because you believe that geniuses are pale and morbid individuals who think all day, never have any fun, and die at an early age, probably as a result of suicide? Lewis Terman carried out a fascinating study to determine whether this sterotype is valid (Terman, 1925; Burks, Jensen, and Terman, 1930; Terman and Oden, 1947; 1959). In 1921 Terman identified over fifteen hundred gifted children, that is, children with IQs of 140 or greater, in the state of California and decided to follow their lives. He found that at birth they weighed an average of twelve ounces more than other babies. They walked, talked, and reached puberty at a younger age, had fewer headaches and hearing defects, and were rated as less nervous than their peers of average intelligence.

During early adulthood they had fewer cases of personality maladjustment, insanity, delinquency, alcoholism, and homosexuality than their average peers. More of them graduated from college, and their representation in the higher professions was eight or nine times their proportional share.

During midlife the mortality rate of the gifted was below that of the general population, and they were also taller. Fewer of them had spent time in mental hospitals or prisons. Ninety percent had entered college, 70 percent graduated, and 22 percent of the men and 5 percent of the women obtained Ph.D.s or M.D.s. Forty-six percent of the men became professionals, and another 41 percent held managerial, official, or semiprofessional jobs. Thus gifted people are not morbid losers. Instead, they have a decided advantage in life. The higher an individual's intelligence, the better off that person is. Other data supporting this conclusion are the positive correlations between intelligence and grades (Frandsen, 1950; Spielberger and Katzenmeyer, 1959), occupational status (Fryer, 1922; Stewart, 1947), and success in psychotherapy (Hiler, 1958; McFarland, Nelson, and Rossi, 1962).

The Neo-Freudian Ego Psychologists

Another group of psychologists who are interested in competence and have approached it from the point of view of psychological adjustment are the neo-Freudian ego psychologists, Erikson, Horney, and Fromm. Freud suggested that personality is composed of three parts: the id, the superego, and the ego. The id is the oldest part of personality and consists of the biological drives, the most important of which are sex and aggression. We discussed the id extensively in the chapter on survival. The superego is the conscience or the internalized rules of society. It consists of prohibitions such as, "Thou shalt not steal, murder, or commit adultery," and prescriptions such as, "Thou shalt love thy neighbor as thyself." Freud felt that conflict between the id and superego is inevitable. The ego is the problem-solving or competency part of personality and does its best to satisfy the demands of the id, the superego, and external reality. Although Freud wrote extensively about the id and the superego, he devoted little time to the ego, which he saw as a mere weak pawn buffeted about by the id, superego, and environmental pressures. He once likened the ego to a man on a runaway horse:

> One might compare the relation of the ego to the id with that between a rider and his horse. The horse provides the locomotive energy, and the rider has the prerogative of determining the goal and of guiding the movements of his powerful mount towards it. But all too often in the relations between the ego and the id we find a picture of the less ideal situation in which the rider is obligated to guide his horse in the direction in which it itself wants to go (Freud, 1933, p. 108).

Freud's followers, however, have not taken such a dim view of the ego. They believe that a strong ego, one that can control the id, superego, and external reality, is possible. Furthermore, they have found evidence that it is essential to psychological health.

Erikson

As noted earlier Erikson theorizes that each stage of development is built around the acquisition of a skill—trust, autonomy, initiative and so on. Thus for Erikson all development is ego development, in other words, competence development. Even id development, which takes place during the trust stage, and superego development, which takes place during the initiative stage, are seen as aspects of ego development.

Horney

When Karen Horney (1939) came to the United States from Germany in 1932, at the height of the depression, she found that most of her patients were suffering from social and economic problems. not psychosexual conflicts. As a result she altered Freud's theory of personality and psychotherapy to give more emphasis to the ego and its relation to the outside world. From her experiences with patients, she concluded that everyone is insecure. Everyone is afraid when it comes to dealing with other people and their environments. To deal with this insecurity the individual can do one of three things. The first option is to run away from the world and become an extreme introvert. The second option is to move against the world through aggression, that is, "getting the other guy before the other guy gets you." The third option is to move toward the world through compliance, that is, "if I'm nice to you, you've got to be nice to me." Each of these attitudes toward other people is effective in some situations and ineffective in others. For studying, moving away is most effective; for playing tennis, moving against is most effective; and for making love, moving with is most effective. Neurotics are locked into a single way of coping, using one strategy whether or not it is effective. Thus if their strategy is to move away, they will spend all of their time with their books and not in competitive sports or dating men or women. Healthy people are able to use all three methods of relating to others and the world. They are able to use all three strategies in coping with their insecurity. Horney's therapy was therefore oriented toward increasing competence, toward helping her patients acquire all three coping styles and learning when to use them.

Fromm

Erich Fromm (1941) was a social psychologist who analyzed the social plight of modern human beings. His conclusions, in a nutshell, are that modern people have tremendous opportunities for freedom and individuality. If, however, they do not develop egos strong enough to create their own security and belongingness, they will be unable to take advantage of these opportunities. I shall present his analysis in some detail below.

Fromm suggests that life can be viewed as a dilemma in which people are torn between security and belongingness, on the one hand, and freedom and individuality, on the other. People can either conform and be like everyone else and thus feel secure and part of a group, or they can rebel and strike out on their own. Each alternative has advantages and disadvantages, but it is very difficult to do both. During the Middle Ages, security and belongingness were easy to obtain while freedom and individuality were almost impossible to attain. The simplicity, homogeneity, and static quality of medieval civilization demanded a minimum number of skills, choices, and adaptions; almost everyone was a farmer, craftsman, or housewife. When the sun came up, everyone would rise: the farmer would go to work in his fields or tend his livestock, the craftsman would go to his shop, and the housewife would cook, clean, mend, and look after the children. Except for minor variations demanded by changing seasons, every day was much like every other day. Almost everyone was a Christian and believed in God, Jesus, and the Virgin Mary. Guilds regulated the quality and price of goods. Each person's life was similar to the life of every other person, and conflict and competition were minimal. Each person was secure and all men and women were brothers and sisters, at least as long as they remained in their home territory.

On the other hand, freedom and individuality could only be attained by becoming an outcast. Serfs were bound to the land. A craftsman had to take up the trade of his father. Believing in something other than the Christian God was heresy, and many witches perished for thinking their own religious thoughts. People took their lives into their own hands if they traveled away from their own home territory.

Fromm likens the Middle Ages to the Garden of Eden and early childhood. In the Garden of Eden, Adam and Eve innocently and blindly followed God's laws. There were no choices, responsibilities, conflicts, or pain and suffering. God was in His heaven and all was right on earth. I can remember the beauty of my own childhood. I played and went to school and whenever I became frightened or confused I would go to my mother or father and they would make everything all right again. I had no purposes or worries. I simply lived from day to day.

In contrast to the Middle Ages, today we are faced with an opposite situation. Individuality and freedom are easy to attain, while security and belongingness are almost impossible to find. The heterogeneity of life-styles and occupations and the geographical and social mobility that characterize modern civilization make individuality and freedom not only easy to obtain but also almost impossible to escape. Science has eliminated many of our myths. There is no longer a hell to fear but also no heaven to which to look forward. Nietzsche and others (Murchland,

1967) have declared that God is dead. We have religious freedom and can follow Billy Graham, the Moonies, Ram Dass, the Hari Krishnas, Zen, Taoism, Sufism, or Tantric yoga. Several hundred religions are available, but with such a wide choice it is difficult to develop faith in any particular one. Religious freedom has given us moral freedom. Today the question is no longer whether premarital sex is moral or immoral but whether or not it should be engaged in on the first date. Scarlet letters are no longer issued for adultery, and bisexuality is being advocated. Science has also given us technology, which has greatly increased our options. Radio, television, and newspapers keep us informed about the latest happenings around the world. Cars and trains and jet airplanes make it possible to travel anywhere and at any time. If the Midwest does not suit you, go to New York City; if the East Coast does not suit you, go to sunny California. If California is not satisfactory, fly to Sweden, Bali, or Katmandu. Modern medicine has almost tripled the lifespan, and it may soon make death obsolete. At the same time, technology has made living much more demanding. To survive in the modern world one has to know how to read and write, type, fill out income tax forms, buy various kinds of insurances, drive on freeways, and balance checking accounts. Furthermore, our technology has created atomic bombs and pollution and is exhausting our natural resources so that life on this planet may cease any day now.

Urbanization has made it possible for everyone to find congenial people, that is, people just like themselves. If you do not like one subculture, you can join another. If you do not like suburban housewives, you can become a motorcycle mama or a go-go dancer or join a group of intellectuals. It is no longer necessary to marry the girl next door. There are thousands of potential spouses from which to choose. But how do you choose from so many? If you make a mistake, it really does not matter because divorce is readily available. In fact, serial monogamy is fast becoming the predominant form of marriage in the United States today. Cities also offer all kinds of events and entertainment: rock concerts, car races, opera, museums, fine restaurants, and gang fights. The anonymity of the city allows people to do pretty much as they please so long as they do not break the law. At the same time, however, cities are lonely. To be loved in a city you have to earn it with your wit, charm, sex appeal, or money. In the country you are part of a family and thus accepted simply for being. In the city people do not interfere with others, but they do not help anyone either. We therefore have events like Kitty Genovese's death, in which thirty-eight people watched from their apartments while her assailant took thirty minutes to stab her to death.

Economic options today are boundless. People can follow any occupation they choose—farmer, lawyer, banker, President of the United States, hippie, hit man for the mob, or housewife or husband. All that is necessary is that they earn the position. Competition for good positions is stiff, and when people can no longer produce, they are terminated. All these things—science, technology, rapid transportation, urbanization, and economic freedom, produce individuality, freedom, insecurity, and loneliness.

Fromm feels that we are often so overwhelmed by our insecurity and loneliness that we long to return to the simplicity of the Middle Ages. The way in which we attempt this return is through authoritarianism; that is, following an external authority. In modern Germany, Italy, and Russia, authoritarianism has taken the form of totalitarian political movements. The Germans became tired of making their own decisions and taking responsibility for their own fate, and thus they decided to have Hitler and the Nazis make their decisions and assume responsibility. It was like returning to childhood again. The Italians made a similar arrangement with Mussolini, and the Russians did the same with the Communists. People living in Western democratic countries have sought to escape the freedom of the modern world through excessive conformity. If you wear blue jeans, eat McDonald's hamburgers, and see the same movies everyone else sees, you know that you are okay. Standing in a crowded bar on Saturday night drinking beer with two hundred other people diminishes your loneliness. Even though the music is so loud that you cannot carry on a conversation, there is "herd warmth." And you know that you are "where it's at" because everyone else is there, too. Everyone is pursuing the latest fad trying to be part of the in crowd. During the 1950s, ducktails, sock hops, and a house and family in suburbia were fashionable. During the 1960s, it was political activism and hippies. During the 1970s, it was Eastern mysticism and spiritualism. No one knows what the next fad will be.

Fromm, however, counsels against authoritarianism (totalitarianism and conformity) because the price it exacts for security and belongingness is loss of freedom and individuality. Loss of freedom and individuality always results in frustration, bitterness, and hatred. The atrocities committed by the Nazis against the Jews were an expression of this frustration, bitterness, and hatred. Instead, Fromm suggests that we embrace our freedom and individuality and develop sufficient ego strength to create our own inner security. He also suggests that people eliminate their loneliness by relating to the world and others through work and love. In this manner it is possible to transcend the dichotomy of security and belongingness versus freedom and individuality and attain the best of both worlds, medieval and modern. Unfortunately, Fromm spends insufficient time describing exactly how the necessary ego strength is to be acquired. He has, however, written an excellent book on love, *The Art of Loving*, which we will discuss later.

Barron's Ego Strength Scale

Systematic research on ego strength began in the 1950s. In 1968, Frank Barron developed a scale to measure ego strength. The scale, which later became the Ego Strength Scale, was initially developed to predict success in psychotherapy. Before beginning psychotherapy, thirty-three psychoneurotics were given the 550 items of the Minnesota Multiphasic Personality Inventory (MMPI). After therapy was terminated, they were rated for improvement by two experts (department heads at the two clinics who participated in the study). An item analysis was then performed on the MMPI items, and those that correlated significantly with improvement were used to make up a scale to predict the success of psychotherapy. Validational research demonstrated that the scale predicted therapy success with other samples of psychoneurotics. The scale was also found to correlate positively with intelligence and ratings of vitality, drive, self-confidence, poise, and breadth of interest and negatively with prejudice and the following clinical scales of the MMPI: Hysteria, Psychasthenia, Schizophrenia, Hypochondriasis, Depression, and Paranoia. On the basis of these data, Barron concluded that the scale measured something broader than potential success in psychotherapy. He concluded that it measured ego strength.

One of the most interesting studies employing the Ego Strength Scale is a study of creative vs. productive writers carried out by Barron (1968). He found that although the creative writers were less psychologically healthy than the productive writers in that the creative writers scored higher on the clinical scales of the MMPI, they were also more healthy in that they scored significantly higher on the Ego Strength Scale. Barron concluded that creative individuals use ego strength to harness their insanity for productive ends.

A study of architects carried out by Barron's colleague, Donald MacKinnon (1973), produced similar results. Forty architects who were selected from all the architects in the United States by their peers as being highly creative were found to score higher on the Ego Strength Scale than either moderately creative or uncreative architects.

Rotter's Internal-External Locus of Control Scale

At the same time that Barron was using psychoanalytic theory to develop the Ego Strength Scale, Julian Rotter was using social learning theory to develop another measure of competence called the Internal-External Locus of Control Scale (Rotter, Chance, and Phares, 1972). Social learning theory states that when an expectation is confirmed the expectation is strengthened and that when it is disconfirmed it is weakened. For example, if I expect laughter when I tell a joke, and the girl that is with me bursts into hysterical laughter when I tell a joke, my expectation that joke telling produces laughter will be strengthened. On the other hand, if I tell a joke and she just keeps watching television as if nothing has happened, my expectation that joke telling produces laughter will be weakened. Expectancies can either be specific, like the belief that putting money in a Coke machine will produce a Coke, or more general, like the belief that moral behavior will ultimately always be rewarded and immoral behavior will always be punished.

One generalized expectancy that greatly affects the learning process itself is the belief that behavior is causally related to outcomes. Some people believe that their behavior determines whether they are rewarded or punished, that is, they believe that they control their outcomes. Other people, however, believe that their outcomes are independent of their behavior. They believe that their outcomes are determined by factors outside their control like fate, luck, and powerful others. Rotter labeled the expectancy that a causal relationship exists between an individual's behavior and outcomes "internal locus of control," and the expectancy that no relationship exists between an individual's behavior and outcomes "external locus of control." People who believe in internal locus of control are called "internals," and people who believe in external locus of control are called "externals." Internals learn instrumental behaviors more rapidly than externals because internals believe that their behavior has effects while externals do not. For example, internal freshmen learn to get good grades much sooner than external freshmen because they believe that their study habits determine their grades, while the external freshmen believe that grades are determined by luck or the kindness (or lack of kindness) of the professors. In general, internals are more competent than externals. Rotter suggested that internal locus of control is similar to White's (1959) concept of competence and Angyal's (1941) concept of autonomy, whereas external locus of control is similar to Seeman's (1959) concept of alienation as it refers to powerlessness.

To measure locus of control, S. Liverant, D. Crowne, and J. Rotter wrote sixty forced-choice items that appeared to measure locus of control. An item analysis was then performed, and items were eliminated if they correlated too highly with a social desirability scale, did not correlate with total score or a validity criterion, or exceeded a response split of 85 percent. The result was a twenty-three-item scale called the Internal-External Locus of Control Scale.

Research using the Internal-External Locus of Control Scale has found that internal locus of control is positively correlated with intelligence, social class, and need for achievement in males and negatively correlated with anxiety. Whites scored more internally than blacks even when social class was controlled; that is, even when the whites and blacks were from the same social class. Peace Corps volunteers scored more internally than the general public. Blacks involved in civil rights activities scored more internally than blacks who were not involved in such activities. High school students planning to attend college scored more internally than high school students not planning to attend college. Nonsmokers were more internal than smokers, and internal smokers who believed the surgeon general's report linking smoking and lung cancer were more likely to quit smoking than external smokers who believed the report. Internal tuberculosis patients were found to know more about their conditions than external patients, and internal prisoners were found to know more about attaining parole than external prisoners. For antecedents, it was found that the parents of internals were more consistent in their application of discipline than parents of externals.

Learned Helplessness and the Sudden Death Phenomenon

Learned Helplessness in Dogs

Recently, syndromes similar to external locus of control, called "learned helplessness" and "the sudden death phenomenon," have been found by the experimental psychologists, Martin Seligman (1975) and C. P. Richter (1958). Seligman was initially interested in avoidance conditioning, a form of conditioning that involves placing a dog into a box containing two compartments separated by a low (shoulder-high) barrier. Each side is equipped with a grid that can be electrified to deliver a shock to the dog. To start conditioning, the dog is placed in one side of the box, a signal is turned on, and then an electric shock is delivered to the dog. Upon receiving the shock, the dog typically yelps and jumps around until it lands on the other side of the barrier where it is safe. After a rest the signal is turned on again, and a little later the dog is shocked. The dog jumps around and eventually escapes to the safe side. After repeated experiences with the signal, the shock, and escape, the dog learns to jump over the barrier when the signal is turned on. In this way the dog avoids being shocked. Seligman's research involved placing dogs in hammocks with holes in them through which their feet hung, attaching electrodes to their feet, turning on a signal, and applying unavoidable shock. Seligman hypothesized that once these dogs were placed in the avoidance conditioning box, they would learn to avoid shock faster than naive dogs that had had no experience with the signal and shock. Much to his surprise, however, his dogs simply cowered in the corner of the box and accepted the shock. They did not learn to avoid the shock. To help the dogs learn to avoid the shock, the barrier was taken down, but this did not help. He then put food on the safe side of the box, but this did not help, either. He then called to the dogs from the safe side of the box. As a result, one of the four dogs learned to avoid the shock after twenty such trials. Finally, Seligman placed ropes around the necks of the remaining dogs and dragged them back and forth from the electrified to the safe side of the box. After twenty, thirty-five, and fifty such trials all of the dogs finally learned to avoid shock.

As a result of this and similar experiments, Seligman concluded that making an organism helpless (for example, giving it unavoidable shock) causes it to learn that it is helpless; the organism acquires the belief that it is helpless. Once this occurs the organism no longer attempts to do anything about its plight. It becomes apathetic and unable to solve problems that it otherwise could. Initially it is anxious, but later depression replaces the anxiety.

Learned Helplessness and People

To find out whether learned helplessness could be produced in human subjects, Donald Hiroto (1974) subjected college students to aversively loud inescapable noise. He then placed them in a situation where moving the hand from one side of a box to the other would turn the noise off. It took the subjects who had been given the unavoidable noise much longer to learn to turn off the noise than subjects who had not experienced the unavoidable noise. He concluded that learned helplessness also occurs in people. Supporting the hypothesis that learned helplessness and the belief in external locus of control are similar phenomena, he found that externals were much more likely to become helpless than internal subjects.

A related experiment carried out by D. C. Glass and J. E. Singer (1972) demonstrated that believing that one has control over a situation, even when this is not true, is better than believing that one is helpless. These experimenters had college students carry out a clerical task while being subjected to loud and unpredictable bursts of sound. Half of the subjects were given a button that they were told they could push to shut off the sound if it became unbearable. They were asked, however, to try to avoid pushing the button. Thus they were led to believe that they had control over the situation. (The button was not actually connected. Fortunately, none of the subjects pushed the button.) The other half of the subjects were not given a button. After this part of the experiment, both groups of subjects attempted to solve puzzles (actually unsolvable) and carry out a proofreading task. It was found that the subjects who had believed that they were in control (had the button) persisted longer in attempting to solve the puzzles and did better on the proofreading task than subjects who had believed that they were helpless (had no button).

Learned Helplessness and Positive Events

In other experiments it has been shown that learned helplessness occurs not only when organisms are subjected to aversive events that they cannot control but also to positive events (Seligman, 1975). In one experiment rats were placed in a Skinner box, and periodically free food was dropped into the box through a hole in its top. These rats were later required to earn their food by pushing a lever. It took these rats longer to learn to push the lever than a group of rats that had not been given the free food. This experiment suggests that welfare states and parents who spoil their children may not be doing their charges favors. Instead, they are teaching them helplessness.

The Sudden Death Phenomenon

At about the same time that Seligman discovered learned helplessness, another experimental psychologist, C. P. Richter (1958), discovered the sudden death phenomenon. Richter's research involved placing wild rats into tanks of water. Although most of the rats would swim for about fifty hours before becoming exhausted and drowning, occasionally a rat would swim around the tank once, dive to the bottom, and die. Autopsies revealed that there was no water in these rats' lungs. These rats had not died of drowning. Richter found that he could increase the probability of the sudden death phenomenon if he held the rat until it became quiescent before placing it in the tank. After observing the sudden death phenomenon again and again, Richter concluded that the rats may have been dying from hopelessness. After having tried unsuccessfully to escape the experimenter's grip and the tank of water, they just gave up and died.

To test the hopelessness hypothesis Richter used a net to dip the rat out of the water tank just as it dove to the bottom to die. In this manner the experimenter communicated to the rat that there was hope. Richter predicted that these rats, when placed back in the water, would swim for the usual fifty hours waiting for the big net to scoop them out. This is indeed what happened.

Although experimental research on the sudden death phenomenon with human subjects has not been carried out (for obvious reasons), observational data exist that suggest that hopelessness does cause death in human beings. One case of sudden death has been reported by H. M. Lefcourt (1973, p. 422):

> This writer witnessed one such case of death due to a loss of will within a psychiatric hospital. A female patient who had remained in a mute state for nearly 10 years was shifted to a different floor of her building along with her floor mates, while her unit was

> redecorated. The third floor of this psychiatric unit where the patient in question had been living was known among the patients as the chronic, hopeless floor. In contrast, the first floor was most commonly occupied by patients who held privileges, including the freedom to come and go on the hospital grounds and to the surrounding streets. In short, the first floor was an exit ward from which patients could anticipate discharge fairly rapidly.
>
> All patients who were temporarily moved from the third floor were given medical examinations prior to the move, and the patient in question was judged to be in excellent medical health though still mute and withdrawn. Shortly after moving to the first floor, this chronic psychiatric patient surprised the ward staff by becoming socially responsive such that within a two-week period she ceased being mute and was actually becoming gregarious. As fate would have it, the redecoration of the third-floor unit was soon completed and all previous residents were returned to it. Within a week after she had been returned to the "hopeless" unit, this patient, who like the legendary Snow White had been aroused from a living torpor, collapsed and died. The subsequent autopsy revealed no pathology of note, and it was whimsically suggested at the time that the patient had died of despair.

In a doctoral dissertation by N. A. Ferrari (1962) fifty-five females, sixty-five years or older, with an average age of eighty-two, were interviewed upon admission to an old age home in the Midwest. They were asked how much freedom of choice they had felt in moving into the home, how many other possibilities had been open to them, and how much pressure had been applied to them to enter the home. Of the seventeen who had no alternative but to enter the old age home, sixteen died unexpectedly within ten weeks of admission. Only one of the thirty-eight women who had alternatives died. Apparently, the women who did not have alternatives died of hopelessness.

Learned Helplessness and Mental Illness

Noting the similarities between learned helplessness (and hopelessness), on the one hand, and a variety of mental illnesses, on the other, Seligman has concluded that they are probably identical. Mental illnesses are simply cases of learned helplessness. Neuroses and psychoses are usually brought on by a problem that the individual cannot solve (helplessness), and they usually result in impaired problem-solving activity, anxiety, depression, and sometimes death.

The Ability to Resist External Pressure

A dimension of personality that is similar to internal locus of control, though not quite identical, is the individual's ability to resist external pressures in decision making. Several individuals have studied this dimension of personality, including David Riesman (1953), Frank Barron (1968), and Herman Witkin (Witkin, Lewis, Hertzman, Machover, Meissner, and Wapner, 1954; 1974).

Inner-Directedness

Riesman, a sociologist, suggests that there are three types of people: tradition-directed, inner-directed, and other-directed. Tradition-directed people are guided by tradition and are usually found in primitive cultures that do not change very much. From Fromm's description of the Middle Ages, we can conclude that medieval people were tradition-directed. Inner-directed people are guided by inner values, and other-directed people are controlled by the opinions of their peers. Inner-directed people are individualists, while other-directed people are conformists. Riesman suggests that the West was won and the United States industrialized by inner-directed people. Today, however, the corporate nature of modern society is causing us to become increasingly other-directed. Evert Shostrom's measure of self-actualization, the Personal Orientation

Inventory, has a measure of inner- versus other-directedness in it.

Independence of Judgment

While Riesman's approach to the ability to resist external pressure is highly theoretical, Barron's approach to this dimension is much more empirical. To select for study people capable of resisting pressures to conform, Barron used a procedure invented by Solomon Asch (1950). This procedure involves telling the subjects that they are participating in a study of perception. They are shown a card containing a standard line and three other lines and instructed to match the standard with one of the other three lines. Before a subject is allowed to answer, however, this subject must listen to the answers of other subjects. Unknown to the real subject, the other subjects are stooges who have been paid by the experimenter to give the wrong answer on twelve of the eighteen trials. Thus for most of the trials the subject is faced with the dilemma of having to choose between giving the right answer and conforming. Asch found that three-quarters of his subjects conformed on at least one trial and 35 percent of all the responses were wrong, owing to conformity.

Some of the situational factors that have been found to influence conformity include privacy (Deutsch and Gerard, 1955), number of stooges (Asch, 1951), and unanimity (Asch, 1951). When judgments were made in private booths, conformity decreased radically. Number of stooges up to three increases conformity. Although as many as sixteen stooges have been used, adding stooges beyond three does not seem to have much of an effect. Unanimity of stooges is very important. If there is only one stooge who gives the correct answer, conformity goes down drastically. Individual differences factors that affect conformity include sex and age (Costanzo and Shaw, 1966). Women are more likely to conform than men, and a curvilinear relationship exists between age and conformity.

Conformity is least for children aged seven to nine. It jumps to its highest point for individuals aged eleven to thirteen and then begins to drop for individuals aged fifteen to seventeen. It drops even further for individuals aged nineteen to twenty-one, though these individuals still conform more than children aged seven to nine.

To study the personality characteristics of "independents" versus "yielders" Barron had several hundred subjects go through the Asch procedure and then selected for further study those who never conformed (independents) and those who conformed on eight or more of the twelve trials (yielders). Forty-six subjects were in each group. The independents and yielders were given the Gough Adjective Checklist, which consists of 279 common personality descriptive adjectives, and were asked to check the adjectives that applied to them. Independents checked the adjectives artistic, emotional, original, demanding, excitable, forgetful, fair-minded, idealistic, logical, mischievous, moody, rational, reckless, and tactless. Yielders checked the adjectives determined, efficient, kind, obliging, optimistic, patient, affected, appreciative, considerate, dignified, enthusiastic, friendly, helpful, humorous, mannerly, modest, stable, tactful, and wise. Barron (1968, pp. 172–73) summarized the factors underlying self-descriptions of the independents as follows:

> (1) a certain positive valuation of intellect and cognitive originality, as well as a spirit of open-mindedness (logical, rational, original, idealistic, fair-minded);
> (2) a high degree of personal involvement and emotional reactivity (emotional, excitable, moody);
> (3) a lack of social ease, or absence of the commonly valued social virtues (tactless, reckless, forgetful, mischievous).

He summarized the factors underlying the self-descriptions of the yielders as follows:

(1) ease and helpfulness in interpersonal relations (kind, obliging, appreciative, considerate, enthusiastic, friendly, helpful, tactful);

(2) personal effectiveness and organization in achieving some goal (determined, efficient, patient, wise).

It was also found that independents were more creative and had a greater preference for complexity than yielders, although no difference in psychological stability was found.

To create a scale for measuring resistance to conformity so that it would not always be necessary to use the awkward Asch procedure, Barron gave his subjects eighty items that he though might measure this dimension of personality. Of these items, twenty-two differentiated independents from yielders, and Barron incorporated these into a scale which he called the Independence of Judgment Scale. After examining the items of this scale Barron (1968) concluded that independents value creative work, personal integrity, independence, intraception, and the challenge of imperfection and contradiction.

A word of caution should be added here. Under some circumstances independence is not an aspect of competence. For example, the rugged individualist who decides to drive a car on the left-hand side of the road is not acting competently (Aronson, 1976).

Psychological Differentiation

Witkin and his associates (1954, 1974) have studied a dimension of personality that he calls "psychological differentiation." Psychological differentiation refers to the extent to which an individual is capable of sorting through a mass of information and responding only to the information that is relevant. If a nondifferentiated person were to come across a rubber snake, he or she would probably run because "a snake is a snake" and one runs away from snakes. On the other hand, if a differentiated person came across a rubber snake, he or she would recognize that it is a toy snake and respond accordingly. This person would probably pick it up and use it to scare friends who were undifferentiated. Witkin has found that undifferentiated individuals do not separate internal from external sources of information and thus are much more susceptible to external influences than are differentiated individuals.

To measure psychological differentiation, Witkin and his associates have developed the Rod and Frame Test, the Body Adjustment Test, and the Embedded Figures Test. The Rod and Frame Test involves presenting an illuminated rod within an illuminated frame to a subject in a dark room. Neither the rod nor the frame is perpendicular and they may or may not be tilted in the same direction. The subject's task is to adjust the rod until it is perpendicular. Differentiated individuals are more successful at this task than nondifferentiated subjects because they are capable of disregarding the distracting frame and working entirely in terms of their own gravitational sense. The Body Adjustment Test involves placing the subject on a tilted chair within a tilted room. The subject is then asked to adjust the chair until he or she is perpendicular. Again, differentiated subjects are more successful in doing this task because they are capable of disregarding the tilted room and working entirely in terms of their own gravitational sense. Because both the Rod and Frame Test and the Body Adjustment Test involve cumbersome equipment, Witkin has developed a paper and pencil measure of differentiation called the Embedded Figures Test. This test consists of twenty-four complex geometrical figures. Within each complex figure a simpler figure has been placed. The subject is shown the complex figure and then the simple figure. After the simple figure has been taken away the subject is again shown the complex figure and asked to find the simple figure in it. Differentiated subjects are more capable of finding the simple figures within the complex figures because they are capable of disregarding distracting lines.

Research on psychological differentiation has shown that men are more differentiated than women and that differentiation increases with age, at least up to age seventeen. Undifferentiated individuals lack self-insight, have low self-esteem, repress feelings and impulses, are passive, conform, and submit to authority. Differentiated individuals are active and independent of their environments, initiate and organize activities and events, and are low in anxiety. In general, differentiated individuals are more competent than nondifferentiated individuals.

Need for Achievement

The last aspect of competence that I am going to discuss is the need for achievement. The need for achievement was initially identified by Henry Murray, who defined it as the "desire or tendency to do things as rapidly and/or as well as possible" (Murray, 1962, p. 164). Most of the work on the need for achievement, however, has been done by David C. McClelland (McClelland, Atkinson, Clark, and Lowell, 1953). McClelland began his research by devising a projective test to measure the need for achievement. This test consists of four pictures: two men in a machine shop, a boy with an open book in front of him, a younger and older man, and a boy with an operation being performed in the background. Subjects are instructed to write stories to accompany the pictures. Using a manual devised by McClelland, the experimenter then picks achievement themes out of the stories. The more achievement themes found in a subject's stories, the higher is the subject's need for achievement score.

The need for achievement has been found to correlate positively with grades (Bendig, 1958), intelligence (Robinson, 1961), preference for high-status jobs (Minor and Neel, 1958), resistance to conformity (Krebs, 1958), delay of gratification (Mischel, 1961), high self-esteem

(Mukherjee and Sinha, 1970), preference for entrepreneurial occupations (McClelland, 1965), and business success (Andrews, 1967).

One of the most interesting aspects of the need for achievement theory is McClelland's (1961) hypothesis that the need for achievement is responsible for successful civilizations. McClelland has found support for this hypothesis from several sources. In one study he counted the number of achievement themes found in children's readers published from 1920 to 1929 in twenty-three different countries and correlated these with economic growth between 1929 and 1950. He found a positive correlation of .53. The greater a country's need for achievement as reflected in its children's literature, the greater was its economic growth. In another study, de Charms and Moeller (1962) counted achievement themes in children's readers (United States) for each year between 1800 and 1950. They then correlated achievement themes with the number of patents issued for each year and obtained a correlation of .79. The greater the number of achievement themes, the greater the number of patents issued. Finally, McClelland (1961) studied the need for achievement and the rise and fall of ancient Greek civilization. By counting achievement themes found in Greek literature, he was able to determine that the need for achievement was highest between 900 B.C. and 475 B.C., declined from 475 B.C. to 362 B.C., and reached a low point from 362 B.C. to 100 B.C. Athenian trade area increased radically during the first period (high need for achievement), peaked during the middle period (declining need for achievement), and shrank radically during the last period (period of lowest need for achievement). For the ancient Greeks, a wave of high need for achievement was followed by a wave of economic and cultural success. Similar results have been found in studies of medieval Spain (Cortes, 1960) and England from the time of the Tudors to the Industrial Revolution (Bradburn and Berlew, in McClelland, 1961).

Let me end this discussion of the need for achievement with a few words of caution. The first is that the need for achievement appears to be a personality trait that only men possess. Although McClelland and his associates (1953) originally collected data on both men and women, they could make no sense out of the women's data and as a result discontinued their research on women. M. Horner (1968) has suggested that women may not have the need for achievement in our culture because they are not encouraged to achieve. Achievement is masculine, and women are punished for doing masculine things. Hopefully, however, the women's movement (and men's liberation) will eventually change this state of affairs. The second warning concerns the need for achievement and psychosomatic illness. Although the need for achievement builds civilizations it also causes psychogenic death. Rudin (1968) correlated McClelland's 1925 need for achievement scores for sixteen countries with the death rates in these nations in 1950. He found that the need for achievement correlated .57 with death from ulcers and .52 with death caused by hypertension. Thus, it may be wise to think twice before developing a high need for achievement.

The Acquisition of Competence

From the data reviewed above, it is obvious that competence (except, possibly, when it takes the form of excessive need for achievement) is a desirable value. The question now is how competence is acquired. To answer this question, we shall first examine how it is formed as a part of normal development and then look at some therapies that can be used to teach competence, if it has not developed normally or has been destroyed.

The Normal Development of Competence

Although Erikson's theory of development suggests that each stage of development involves mastering a new task and thus increasing one's competence, the stages of autonomy, initiative, and industry deal with the basic kind of competence discussed in this chapter. As noted earlier, autonomy is acquired during the second and third years. To help children acquire autonomy, they should be supported in their efforts toward independence. Parents should not view the negativism of their two-year-old as rejection or an indication that they are raising a psychopathic deviant, but rather should be pleased that the child is learning to take care of him or herself. At the same time, parents should not become the slaves of their two-year-old. Although the two-year-old is not yet capable of realizing that the world was not created entirely for his or her happiness, it was not. To perpetuate this illusion by conforming to it is not doing any child a favor. A few rules that are firmly and consistently enforced are important even at this stage of development.

Initiative is acquired during the fourth and fifth years. During this stage the autonomy acquired during the previous stage is combined with sexual curiosity to create a very active child. To channel this activity, a conscience must be developed that is strong enough to allow the child to effectively (cooperatively) interact with others but yet not be too strong. If the conscience is too strong it will destroy initiative because of pervasive guilt. To create a healthy conscience, Erikson suggests that parents put together a set of reasonable rules and then consistently enforce them.

A personality theorist who has placed special emphasis on this stage of development is Otto Rank, a disciple of Freud who later broke with him. Like Fromm, Rank felt that in living, people must choose either a conventional existence (security and belongingness) or one that involves autonomy and creativity (freedom and individuality). The choice of a conventional or creative life depends to a large extent on how people have been socialized. Parents who force strict obedience from their children produce adapted, conventional children, that is, children with overly strong consciences. On the other hand, parents who view their children as separate human beings with their own wants and needs, and interact with them on this basis, tend to produce autonomous, creative children. MacKinnon's (1973) research on creative architects, referred to earlier, supports Rank's theorizing. MacKinnon found that the noncreative architects were much more heavily socialized than the creative architects.

Industry is acquired during the early school years. During this period children must acquire the basic skills necessary to become productive members of society. Teachers play a more important role in helping children achieve industry than do parents. A sense of industry is most easily acquired when teachers can demonstrate to children the relevance of the skills they are acquiring for adult living.

One study that has looked carefully at the development of competence is Stanley Coopersmith's (1967) study of self-esteem in boys, eight to ten years of age. Although competence and self-esteem are not necessarily identical concepts, for boys of this age they probably are. The more competent a boy is, the greater is his pride in himself, that is, self-esteem. Coopersmith studied how parent characteristics, child characteristics, and child-rearing practices affected self-esteem. With respect to parent characteristics, he found that the mothers of high self-esteem boys had higher self-esteems and were emotionally more stable than mothers of medium- or low self-esteem boys. These results suggest that the high self-esteem boys modeled the self-esteems of their mothers. With respect to personal characteristics, the high self-esteem boys were found to have higher IQs and lower anxiety scores than the medium- or low self-esteem boys. Furthermore, the low self-esteem boys were found to be below average in physique. These results suggest that if people are born with socially desirable characteristics, it is easier for them to think highly of themselves than if they have not been born with such characteristics. In terms of child-rearing practices, it was found that high self-esteem boys were shown more affection than moderate- or low self-esteem boys. They were also raised in democratic homes, which are homes in which children are respected as separate individuals and given freedom to do what they want within a set of reasonable rules that are consistently and firmly enforced. Rule enforcement for the high self-esteem boys more frequently took the form of management (for example, reasoning, separation, or distraction) than withdrawal of love or corporal punishment. In general, these child-rearing practices are similar to those recommended by Erikson and Rank. Self-esteem, the subjective side of competence, appears to be the result of superior talent (high IQ, psychological stability, and good physique) and "proper" socialization (parental modeling of high self-esteem, love, and a democratic home environment).

Unlike some of the other aspects of competence (for example, ego-strength or internal locus of control), several studies have been carried out on the child-rearing practices that affect the need for achievement. McClelland and his associates (1953) found that boys with a high need for achievement described their parents as more severe than boys with a low need for achievement. They described their parents as autocratic, rejecting, unprotective, unsolicitous, neglectful, and rigid. Cox (1962, cited in Byrne, 1974) found that boys with a high need for achievement had more household duties and responsibilities than boys with a low need for achievement. Winterbottom (1958) found that mothers of boys with a high need for achievement taught their sons various independence tasks at an earlier age than mothers of boys with a low need for achievement. Some of the independence tasks included: "to know his way around his part of the city so he can play where he wants without getting lost," "to take part in his parents' interests and conversations," "to be able to undress and go to bed by himself," and "to earn his own spending money." Winterbottom also found that mothers of boys with a high need for achievement rewarded their sons' achievements with physical affection (hugs and kisses). Finally, Rosen and D'Andrade (1959) visited the homes of boys with high and low needs for achievement, respectively, and had them perform tasks, like tossing rings over a peg, in the presence of their parents. They found that the parents of boys with a high need for achievement set higher goals for their sons and had greater confidence in them than the parents of the boys with a low need for achievement. Furthermore, the parents of the boys with a high need for achievement were more involved in the tasks and praised their sons when they succeeded but showed disapproval when they failed. Thus, to bring up boys to have high needs for achievement, be severe, give them numerous household duties and responsibilities, teach them to be independent, reward their successes with hugs and kisses and punish their failures with disapproval, hold great expectations for them, and have confidence in them. On the other hand, to bring up easygoing boys, make life easy for them. Do not give them responsibilities or push them to become independent. Give them love not only when they succeed but also when they fail. Let them know that they are loved for being, not performing.

Curing Learned Helplessness

If competence has not been acquired by adolescence or has been destroyed, what then? A number of therapies have been developed to help people acquire competence. These therapies include behavior therapies, assertiveness training, reality therapy, rational-emotive therapy, and need for achievement training. In reviewing these therapies, I shall first discuss the work of Seligman. As part of his research on learned helplessness, Seligman (1975) has investigated ways of preventing and curing this condition. He has found that the best way to prevent learned helplessness is to teach the organism that it is competent. An experiment that demonstrated this point involved placing dogs in a shuttle box (the box with the two compartments described earlier) and teaching them to avoid shock. These dogs were then given unavoidable shock in the hammocks and then placed back in the shuttle boxes. Unlike the dogs that just received unavoidable shock, these animals did not become helpless. When they were placed in a situation where they could avoid shock, they did.

A variation of this experiment was carried out by C. S. Dweck (1972). This experiment involved three groups of children. One group received training with simple math problems, problems that the children could almost always answer correctly. The second group received training with math problems, half of which were very simple and half of which were almost impossible to solve. When the children in this group failed to solve a problem, they were taught to attribute the failure to themselves. They were told that they had failed because they had not tried hard enough. In this group the children were not only taught that they could succeed but also how to manage failure. The third group of children received no training with math problems at all. After the training was completed, all three groups of children were given moderately difficult problems to solve. It was found that the children in the second group persisted longer and solved more problems than subjects in either of the other two groups. Learning that they were not helpless in the face of difficulty enabled them to manage the difficult situation. In general, the more experience and skills a person can acquire the less susceptible to learned helplessness that person will become. Taking calculus, learning how to ride motorcycles and wild horses, traveling around Europe, and taking dancing lessons are all ways of immunizing one's self against learned helplessness.

To cure learned helplessness, Seligman found that it was necessary to demonstrate to the organism that it was not helpless. This is often not an easy task because the organism has given up. It no longer looks for ways of controlling its situation, and when ways are presented it often does not attempt to grasp them. As noted earlier, to cure dogs of learned helplessness, Seligman had to literally drag them back and forth from the electrified to the safe side of the shuttle box. The motivational and cognitive decrements that result from learned helplessness probably explain why psychotherapy is often such a long and arduous process.

E. P. Burgess (1968) has developed a therapy similar to "dog dragging" for human patients suffering from depression. This therapy involves having patients engage in various graded tasks. As depressed patients are "forced" to accomplish more and more of these tasks, they eventually discover that they are not helpless. They discover that they can exert some control over their environment and as a result their depression disappears.

Experimental Neuroses

Although Seligman's discovery of animal neurosis (learned helplessness) was surprising to him, he was not the first to discover animal neurosis. In 1927 Ivan Pavlov published a paper in which he described animal maladjustment, labeling it "experimental neurosis." He taught a dog to salivate to an ellipse but not a circle. He then began "fattening" the ellipse and flattening the circle until he presented a figure halfway between the original ellipse and circle. Then the dog did not know whether or not to salivate, and it became highly disturbed. It became very emotional, lost its ability to make simpler discriminations, and became intensely afraid of the experimental apparatus. H. S. Liddell (1948, 1953) discovered a similar phenomenon in sheep when he restricted them in a harness and required them to make a large number of classically conditioned responses. J. H. Masserman (1943) created experimental neuroses in cats by placing them in an approach-avoidance conflict situation. After the cats had been conditioned to lift the lid of a food box and eat when a signal was given, Masserman rigged the food box so that the cats would receive a blast of air (an aversive stimulus) when the lid was opened. The cats became highly disturbed by this situation, responding with agitation or immobilized vocalization, refusal of food, and sensitivity to extraneous stimuli. Finally a South African psychiatrist, J. Wolpe (1953, 1957), has used experimentation with animal neuroses to create a therapy for human neuroses. After reviewing the literature on experimental neurosis, Wolpe concluded that neurosis is simply a case of conditioned fear. Pavlov conditioned his dog to fear the experimental situation by requiring it to make an impossible discrimination; Liddell conditioned his sheep to fear the experimental situation by restraining them and requiring them to make a large number of conditioned responses; and Masserman conditioned his cats to fear their food box by subjecting them to an approach-avoidance conflict. To demonstrate that experimental neurosis is simply conditioned fear, Wolpe placed cats in a cage and gave them electric shocks. Thereafter, whenever Wolpe placed the cats in the cage he got the typical neurotic reaction involving "various combinations of the following symptoms—rushing hither and thither, getting up on the hind legs, clawing at the floor, roof, and sides of the experimental cage, crouching, trembling, howling, spitting; hydriasis, rapid respiration, piloerection, and in some cases, urination and defecation" (1957, p. 254).

Having demonstrated that neurosis is a matter of conditioned fear, Wolpe decided that to cure neurosis the fear response must be eliminated. To accomplish this Wolpe devised the strategy of conditioning responses incompatible with fear to the stimuli that elicited the fear. To cure his neurotic cats Wolpe decided to condition eating, which is incompatible with fear, to the cage where the cats received the electric shocks. To accomplish this he initially induced the cats to eat at some distance from the cage. Then he gradually reduced the distance until they were eating in the cage itself. After this the cats evidenced no fear of the cage; their neuroses had been cured.

In many ways the analyses of experimental neuroses of Seligman and Wolpe are highly similar. Both believe maladjustment is the result of a traumatic event. (Seligman's spoiled children and victims of a welfare state do not become maladjusted until after they are required to earn their own keep, a fairly traumatic event.) Both believe that the traumatic event is followed by a debilitating response—learned helplessness or fear. And both believe that the cure for maladjustment is found in removing the debilitating response by demonstrating that the situation is no longer traumatizing—demonstrating that the cage is no longer electrified (Wolpe) or that the shock can be avoided (Seligman).

Systematic Desensitization

On the basis of his animal research, Wolpe (1958) has developed an extensive therapy to be used with human patients. Like his treatment of animal neurosis, Wolpe conditions responses that are incompatible with fear to the stimuli that elicit the fear. One specific technique that Wolpe has developed to accomplish this end is systematic desensitization. Systematic desensitization involves interviewing the patient to find out which situations produce fear. These situations are then arranged into a hierarchy from least to greatest. An example of such a hierarchy is the following, assembled for a patient who feared death and its accoutrements: seeing an ambulance, seeing a hospital, being inside a hospital, reading the obituary notice of an older person, passing a funeral home, seeing a funeral, driving past a cemetery, reading the obituary notice of a young person who had died of a heart attack, seeing a burial assemblage from afar, being at a burial, and seeing her first husband in his coffin (Sundberg and Tyler, 1962). The patient is then taught a response that is incompatible with fear, such as relaxation, sexual arousal, or assertiveness. While the patient is experiencing the response that is incompatible with fear, the patient is asked to imagine the least fearful event in his or her fear hierarchy. The therapist and patient then work their way up the hierarchy until the patient signals that he or she is feeling fear. During following sessions they work their way farther and farther up the hierarchy until the patient's fears are gone. Remarkably good transfer from imagined to real situations has been found. A wide variety of different kinds of hierarchies has been constructed. In his book on personality assessment, Walter Mischel (1968) described a guilt hierarchy that was constructed for a patient suffering from excessive guilt, and I once helped a student construct a hierarchy for dealing with fear of demon possession. A number of research projects that compared systematic desensitization with traditional forms of therapy found it equal or superior to traditional therapies (for example, Paul, 1966; 1967). Systematic desensitization helps people increase their competence by ridding them of debilitating fears.

Assertiveness Training

A recent movement that is oriented toward increasing personal competence and has some of its roots in behavior therapy is the assertiveness training movement. (It also has roots in the women's movement.) Alberti and Emmons (1974), who published one of the first books on assertiveness, state that the goal of assertiveness training is to help individuals overcome feelings of personal insignificance in the modern world. (This goal is highly compatible with Fromm's diagnosis of the needs of people today.) One of the basic assumptions is that all people are equal in worth and thus have the right to express themselves, providing that in so doing they do not interfere with the rights of others. Doctors are not better than plumbers; parents are not better than children; winners are not better than losers. Alberti and Emmons differentiate assertiveness from nonassertiveness and aggression. Assertive people view all people, including themselves, as equals while nonassertive people view others as better than themselves and aggressive people view others as inferior to themselves.

Assertiveness training takes place in small groups of ten to twelve persons who meet biweekly for eight to ten weeks. In these groups, individuals practice being assertive. Assertiveness training begins by having the individual pick out specific instances in which he or she does not behave assertively. The individual then figures out assertive responses to these situations and imagines him or herself making these responses. After this, the individual role-plays the assertive responses and then, finally, actually tries them out. At each stage the individual monitors the effectiveness of his or her assertiveness, seeks feedback from others, and makes any changes that appear to be necessary. Alberti and Emmons aim primarily at behavior change, assuming that attitude change will follow, and depend on the intrinsic superiority of assertive (competent) interpersonal behavior to provide the reinforcement necessary for its maintenance.

Reality Therapy

William Glasser's (1975) reality therapy is another form of competence therapy. Glasser suggests that neurotics, psychotics, and psychopaths all have one thing in common: they are unable to satisfy their needs in a realistic manner. They are incompetent. Because they are unsuccessful in satisfying their needs, they are often anxious and depressed. A second characteristic of these three classes of people is that they are irresponsible. They refuse to recognize their own needs and acquire the skills necessary for their satisfaction. Instead they have chosen some form of escape. Neurotics deal with their needs by repressing them, denying external reality, and using other defense mechanisms. Psychotics withdraw into a world of fantasy, and psychopaths blame other people for their frustrations and obtain gratification by ignoring the rights of others. The goal of reality therapy is to help neurotics, psychotics, and psychopaths take responsibility for their needs and learn the skills needed to obtain their satisfaction. These ends are accomplished by a process that resembles socialization. Initially, the therapist builds a warm and accepting relationship with the client. If the therapist does not really care about the client, reality therapy will not work. After building a warm relationship with the client, the therapist begins to encourage the client to become responsible for his or her needs and learn how to satisfy them. As a result of the warmth combined with the demand for responsible behavior, the client is placed in a bind. Clients have to choose either to continue to accept the therapist's concern and become responsible for the satisfaction of their needs or reject the therapist and maintain their irresponsible ways. If the therapist's concern is genuine and the demands sincerely and firmly maintained, the therapy is usually successful. Reality therapy is different from some therapies in that it is almost entirely oriented to the present and future. The client's childhood is not discussed. Instead, the individual is encouraged to develop future goals and ways of attaining these goals.

Reality therapy has been implemented by Glasser at Ventura, a treatment facility for delinquent girls in California. Glasser (1975, p. 83) described the program as follows:

> 1. *The Custody Program* is administered by warm and skillful counselors who use the principles of Reality Therapy. The girl's knowledge that she is in an institution from which she cannot escape is basic to the program. With the guidance of the staff, she is forced to take the responsibility for her behavior in a total situation where responsibility is continually stressed.
>
> 2. *The Treatment Program* is administered by a group of competent psychologists, social workers, and a consulting psychiatrist. The treatment personnel not only work with the girls directly, but they continu-

ally work with the custody staff to help them treat the girls according to the principles of Reality Therapy.

3. *The School Program* consists of both academic and vocational courses taught by qualified teachers. All girls have a full daily schedule taking either an academic or a vocational course, or sometimes both. Those who enter the Ventura School with sufficient credits and who stay long enough and complete enough work to graduate receive a regular graduation certificate which does not indicate that it comes from a correctional institution.

The success rate at Ventura is about 80 percent. A colleague of Glasser, G. L. Harrington, has applied reality therapy to hospitalized psychotics. Before Harrington took over Building 206 of the Veterans Administration Neuropsychiatric Hospital in West Los Angeles, the 210 patients housed there and the staff lived a symbiotic existence. The staff gave the patients tender loving care, and the patients gave up acting crazy and making trouble. Only about two patients were discharged each year. When Harrington took over the building he taught reality therapy to the staff and divided the building into three wards, a fifty-man closed ward, a fifty-man semiopen ward, and a hundred-man open ward. Patients were assigned to one of the three wards depending on how irresponsible and "crazy" they acted. On the closed ward, the staff began working with the patients to encourage them to take minimal responsibility for their own care. That is, patients were encouraged to eat, bathe, shave, brush their teeth, change clothes, and take needed medication. When the patient acquired these skills, he was moved to the semiopen ward where he attended group meetings and did at least one hour of ward detail per day. Later he was given a grounds card, which entitled him to go outside for recreation and work. As the patient became more and more self-sufficient, his self-esteem rose and he began to act like a human being. After ninety days the patient was moved to the open ward, where he prepared to leave the hospital. After ninety days on the open ward, the patient was sent out into the community to live, often returning during the day to work and receive the support of the hospital. Finally, the patient looked for work in the community. As a result of reality therapy, twenty-five patients were released in 1962, seventy-five in 1963, and it was estimated that two hundred per year would be released in the next two years.

Rational-Emotive Therapy

Albert Ellis's (1977) rational-emotive therapy (RET) is a competency therapy that is oriented toward combating irrational, self-defeating thoughts. Ellis suggests that maladjustment is not the product of unfortunate external events, like losing a job, flunking out of school, or having cancer. Instead, he believes it is a product of the way in which people interpret events. If they interpret events rationally, they may feel disappointment, sorrow, regret, frustration, or annoyance, but they will never feel anxiety, depression, or worthlessness. The latter feelings accompany maladjustment, which is produced by irrational thinking.

Rational-emotive therapy is oriented toward helping the neurotic get rid of irrational beliefs. One of the devices Ellis (1977) has created for this is a list of twenty-seven irrational beliefs. This list is presented in Table 4.1. To improve your psychological health, you may want to go through this list and make sure that you do not hold any of these beliefs. Simply memorizing this list and refusing to hold any of these beliefs, however, is not as effective as understanding the irrationality in each of the beliefs. Being able to discriminate rational from irrational thought will allow you to deal with events not covered by Ellis's list, which is, of necessity, limited.

With respect to the effectiveness of rational-emotive therapy, Ellis himself has found it quite useful. Initially, Ellis practiced orthodox psychoanalysis. He then moved to psychoanalytically oriented psychotherapy and, finally, invented rational-emotive therapy. In evaluating the cases completed under each of the kinds of therapy, he found that with orthodox psychoanalysis, 50 percent of his clients showed little or no improvement, 37 percent showed some distinct improvement, and only 13 percent showed considerable improvement. With analytically oriented psychotherapy, 37 percent showed little or no improvement, 45 percent showed some distinct improvement, and 18 percent showed considerable improvement. With rational-emotive therapy, 10 percent showed little or no improvement, 46 percent showed some distinct improvement, and 44 percent showed considerable improvement.

After a thorough review of all the outcome studies done on rational-emotive therapy, Raymond DiGiuseppe and Norman Miller (1977) concluded that it is effective. Specifically, they found that:

> (1) rational-emotive therapy is more effective than client-centered therapy with introverted persons;
> (2) it is more effective than systematic desensitization in the reduction of general or pervasive anxiety;
> (3) a combination of cognitive therapy and behavior therapy appears to be the most efficacious treatment for depression;
> (4) the relative effectiveness of rational-emotive therapy versus assertiveness training is inconclusive due to limited and confounded research (DiGiuseppe and Miller, 1977, p. 89).

Increasing Need for Achievement

After having read about the studies that demonstrated that a high need for achievement is responsible for successful civilizations, it may be interesting to know whether or not there is a therapy for increasing the need for achievement. Fortunately, there is. R. W. Burris (1958) carried out a study that involved three groups of subjects equated for need for achievement. One group met for eight weeks, forty minutes per week, to practice writing stories containing achievement themes. The second group met for eight weeks for counseling on how to study, and the third group did not meet at all. At the end of the eight weeks all three groups again took the need for achievement test, and it was found that the first group significantly increased their scores, while the other two groups did not. Burris also looked at the grade-point averages of the groups for the following semester and found a significant increase in grades for the first group but not for the other two groups.

McClelland and D. C. Winter (1969) have sought to teach the acquisition of the need for achievement to businessmen and have had some success. Their program, which involved achievement imagery, role-playing, group activities, and interpretation of cultural values according to the need for achievement, was carried out with businessmen in two Indian cities. After the program they found an increase in business activity, hours spent in work, new business ventures, capital investments, employment of other people, and gross income for the businessmen who participated in the program.

Nonattachment, Passivity, and Fatalism

In discussing competence thus far, we have focused entirely on Western pragmatism, a go-out-and-get-'er-done kind of competence. What about the Eastern concept of nonattachment, feminine passivity (taking time to smell the roses), or even fatalism? Are all of these traits bad because they did not help us win the West? I do not think so. I feel that they, too, have value and are in fact other aspects of competence. Nonattachment is the method by which the Hindu and Buddhist seek to live the good life on earth and attain moksha, or release from further reincarnations (McCasland, Cairns, and Yu, 1969). Moksha results in nonconscious unity with God or eternal bliss, depending upon which school of belief is followed. Nonattachment involves getting rid of all desires. It involves realizing that all things are simply illusions and thus cannot be attained, at least not permanently. It is wise, therefore, not to desire them in the first place. Nonattachment appears to be another strategy for dealing with needs. Westerners handle their needs by rushing out to satisfy them whenever they arise, while Easterners deal with needs by eliminating them through self-discipline. For example, Westerners deal with the need for warmth in the winter and coolness in the summer by building insulated buildings with furnaces and air conditioning. On the other hand, the Hindu or Buddhist seeks to eliminate the need for heat or air conditioning through self-discipline. Both heat and cold are viewed as illusions. One hundred degrees is viewed as hot and aversive until the temperature rises to 125 degrees. Then 100 degrees is nostalgically remembered as cool and pleasant. Since heat and cold are illusions, they can be ignored, and the Hindu holy man wears nothing but a loin cloth, year round. Both strategies for dealing with needs, that is, seeking their satisfaction and seeking their elimination, are aspects of competence. Both Eastern and Western strategies involve a great deal of effort. Westerners work a forty- to seventy-hour week to afford the products required to satisfy their needs, while Hindus follows one of the four yogas (knowledge, work, love, or raja yoga) and Buddhists practice the Eightfold Path (right knowledge, right thought, right speech, right conduct, right livelihood, right efforts, right mindfulness, and right concentration).

A combination of Eastern and Western strategies would seem to be optimal. Self-discipline should be used to limit needs to only those that the individual feels are really important; these needs should then be satisfied through effective interaction with the external world.

Passivity involves being quiet and appreciating the events that are taking place inside one's mind and body and in the world outside. It involves smelling roses, appreciating good rhythm and blues music, touching soft velvet and stiff denim, and being able to taste the difference between Schlitz and Coors beer. It involves feeling the ecstasy of first love, the darkness when it ends, and the mature hope after the darkness. It also involves empathizing with the pain of a friend whose father is critically ill, the delight of a baby playing with his toes, and the happiness of a classmate who has just been accepted for graduate work at MIT. Although being aware of one's inner and outer environment often serves no ulterior purpose, the information gathered through passive awareness forms the basis for effective action. It indicates what needs to be done, how to do it, and after the action is completed, whether the activity was effective or satisfying. Activity that does not flow from passive receptivity is useless. Robert Ornstein (1972), in his book, *The Psychology of Consciousness*, makes this particularly clear. Ornstein presents evidence suggesting that the left hemisphere of the brain is active, day-oriented, intellectual, concerned with time, explicit, analytic, propositional, linear, sequential, focal, masculine, verbal, causal, and argumentative. On the other hand, the right hemisphere is passive (receptive), night-oriented, sensuous, eternal, tacit, gestalt, oppositional, nonlinear, simultaneous, diffuse, feminine, dark, spatial, intuitive, acausal, and experiential. Competence is composed of both right and left hemispheric functioning. Passivity, in the form of sleep, meditation, or simple relaxation, is also important for recuperation after activity.

Fatalism is the belief that the individual is powerless, that is, what is going to happen will inevitably happen. It reflects an extremely external view of life. Although most men, particularly if they have been raised on John Wayne movies, would rather die than admit that there is anything that they cannot do, the truth of the matter is that there are probably more things against which they are powerless than they can control. Men have little control over cancer, hurricanes, floods, schizophrenia, inflation, government bureaucracies, or war. And even if we conquer everything else, there is always death. In dealing with events that are beyond our control, fatalism would seem to be adaptive. It is probably better to admit our powerlessness than to continually attempt to control a situation and fail. Camille Wortman, Lawrence Panicera, Lisa Shusterman, and J. Hibscher (1976) carried out an experiment that supports this conclusion. In this experiment, subjects were caused either to succeed or fail at a task. Half of those failing were led to believe that they had failed because of their own incompetence, while the other half were led to believe that they had failed because the task was impossible. In other words, half of the subjects were led to adopt a nonfatalistic attitude, and the other half were led to adopt a fatalistic attitude. It was found that the nonfatalists experienced more stress than the fatalists. In fact, the stress experienced by the fatalists was no more than the "stress" experienced by the successful subjects. Other data supporting the notion that fatalism is useful in some situations come from Kübler-Ross's (1970) research with the dying. Kübler-Ross found that people who die happily are people who no longer deny or fight their approaching death but accept it. Competent individuals invest their time, energy, and resources into situations in which their investment will do the most good. They accept the impossible and do not waste their resources trying to change it. They live by the prayer of Alcoholics Anonymous: "Oh God, give us the serenity to accept what cannot be changed, courage to change what should be changed, and wisdom to distinguish the one from the other."

TABLE 4.1*

TWENTY-SEVEN IRRATIONAL BELIEFS

1. I must have sincere love and approval almost all the time from the people I find significant.

---

*Reprinted from Albert Ellis and Russell Grieger, eds., *Handbook of Rational-Emotive Therapy*, pp. 12-14. Copyright © 1977 by Springer Publishing Company, Inc., New York. Used by permission.

2. I must prove myself thoroughly competent, adequate, and achieving, or at least have real competence or talent at something important.
3. My emotional misery comes almost completely from external pressures that I have little ability to change or control; unless these pressures change, I cannot help making myself feel anxious, depressed, or hostile.
4. If events occur that put me in real danger or that threaten my life, I have to make myself exceptionally preoccupied with and upset about them.
5. My past life influenced me immensely and remains all-important because if something once strongly affected me it has to keep determining my feelings and behavior today; my early childhood gullibility and conditionability still remains, and I cannot surmount it and think for myself.
6. I must have a high degree of order or certainty in the universe around me to enable me to feel comfortable and to perform adequately.
7. I desperately need others to rely and depend upon; because I shall always remain so weak, I also need some supernatural power on which to rely, especially in times of severe crisis.
8. I must understand the nature or secret of the universe in order to live happily in it.
9. I can and should give myself a global rating as a human, and I can only rate myself as good or worthy if I perform well, do worthwhile things, and have people generally approve of me.
10. If I make myself depressed, anxious, ashamed, or angry, or I weakly give in to the feelings of disturbance that people and events tend to make me feel, I perform most incompetently and shamefully. I must not do that, and I amount to a thoroughly weak, rotten person if I do.

11. Beliefs held by respected authorities or by my society must prove correct and I have no right to question them in theory or action; if I do, people have a perfect right to condemn and punish me, and I cannot bear their disapproval.
12. Others must treat everyone in a fair and just manner; and if they act unfairly or unethically they amount to rotten people, deserve damnation and severe punishment, and justice will almost certainly see that they get this kind of retribution.
13. If others behave incompetently or stupidly, they turn into complete idiots and ought to feel thoroughly ashamed of themselves.
14. If people have the ability to do well but actually choose to shirk and avoid the responsibilities they should accept and carry out, they amount to rotters and should feel utterly ashamed of themselves. People must achieve their full potential for happy and worthwhile living, else they have little or no value as humans.
15. Things must go the way I would like them to go, because I need what I want; and life proves awful, terrible, and horrible when I do not get what I prefer.
16. When dangers or fearsome people or things exist in my world, I must continually preoccupy myself about them; in that way I will have the power to control or change them.
17. I find it easier to avoid facing many of life's difficulties and self-responsibilities than to undertake more rewarding forms of self-discipline. I need immediate comfort and cannot go through present pain to achieve future gain.
18. People should act better than they usually do; and if they don't act well and do create needless hassles for me, I view it as awful and horrible and I can't stand the hassles that they then create.

19. Once handicaps exist in my life, either because of my hereditary tendencies or the influences of my past or present environment, I can do practically nothing to change them; I must continue to suffer endlessly because of these handicaps. Therefore life hardly seems worth continuing.
20. If changing some obnoxious or handicapping element in myself or my life proves hard, that difficulty ought not exist. I find it *too* hard to do anything about it; I might as well make no effort, or very little effort, to change it.
21. Things like justice, fairness, equality, and democracy clearly have to prevail; when they don't, I can't stand it and life seems too unbearable to continue.
22. I must find correct and practically perfect solutions to my problems and others' problems; if I don't, catastrophe and horror will result.
23. People and external events cause practically all my unhappiness and I have to remain a helpless victim of anxiety, depression, feelings of inadequacy, and hostility unless these conditions and people change and allow me to stop feeling disturbed.
24. Since I managed to get born and now remain alive, my life has to continue forever, or just about as long as I want it to continue. I find it completely unfair and horrible to think about the possibility of my dying and no longer having any existence.
25. As long as I remain alive, my life has to have some unusual or special meaning or purpose; if I cannot create this meaning or purpose for myself, the universe or some supernatural force in the universe must give it to me.
26. I can't stand the discomfort of feeling anxious, depressed, guilty, ashamed, or otherwise emotionally upset; if I really went crazy and wound up in a mental institution, I never could stand that horror and might well have to kill myself.

27. When things have really gone bad for me for a reasonably long period of time and no guarantee exists that they will change or that anyone will take over my life and make things better for me, I simply can't bear the thought of living any longer and have to seriously consider killing myself.

5. Self-Enhancement

After people have acquired enough competencies to make their long-range survival secure and they have time, energy, and resources left over, they become interested in self-enhancement. Self-enhancement involves both discovering and creating their selves. It involves exploring the physiological equipment that people have inherited from their parents and using this raw material and input from the environment to create extensive modifications.

The Importance of Self-Enhancement

Self-enhancement is a luxury in that it involves the expenditure of time, energy, and resources to accomplish things that have little or no value for survival. Self-enhancing individuals treat themselves like sculptors treat their clay or stamp collectors treat their collections. They are continuously building, expanding, and modifying themselves. They spend hours reading books and going to movies and plays looking for heros or heroines to copy. They put much effort into programs like TM, TA, EST, and wilderness survival school. They make New Year's resolutions, promise themselves that they will get out of old ruts, and write five-year plans for self-improvement. They spend money on appurtenances to help them become the kind of people they wish to be—hairstyles, pets, clothes and jewelry, housing, art, cars, and recreational equipment. Much of their happiness comes from observing the progress they are making toward the attainment of their ideal self, and much of their sorrow is created by their shortcomings in this struggle. All these activities, though tremendously important and appropriate, have little to do with survival.

Individuals seeking short- and long-term survival (competence) are similar, in many ways, to each other because they are all guided by the same general constraints. They all seek food, water, sleep, sex, and protection and the skills needed to insure that these commodities will continue to be readily available. Everyone eats, sleeps, copulates, defecates, and fights in pretty much the same manner. In contrast, individuals seeking self-enhancement are significantly different from each other. There are as many different kinds of self-enhancement as there are individuals. This is because very few constraints apply to self-enhancement. Self-enhancement does not involve universal goals or methods for attaining these goals. Although it is possible to tell people that to survive they must eat, it is impossible to tell people what type of life-style will be right for them. Each person has to discover this independently, and each outcome is unique.

The change from similarity (survival, competence) to uniqueness (self-enhancement) occurs as people move from childhood into adolescence. During childhood each child is quite similar to every other child, at least within a given culture. They play the same games, watch the same TV programs, learn the same things at school, and pass through the same grades at more or less the same rate. With adolescence, however, divergence begins, and self-exploration becomes possible. In fact, it becomes a necessity. In high school, some students follow college prep tracks while others follow tracks that lead to terminal degrees. After high school, some people go to college while others seek jobs. Within college a variety of different majors are available, and after graduation from high school or college, thousands of different job possibilities become available. Although self-enhancement is undoubtedly a process that continues throughout the individual's lifetime, the bulk of it is normally accomplished during the adolescent years. During these years individuals become attuned to the more or less enduring aspects of their personalities and make decisions that fix the broad outlines of their lives.

Self-enhancement corresponds to the fulfillment of Maslow's belongingness and esteem needs. Once individuals have acquired a sense of security, they seek to develop a personality that is acceptable to others (belongingness) and of which they and others can be proud (esteem). Self-enhancement corresponds to Erikson's stage of identity achievement. Although individuals have an identity before this stage (they are male or female, are a certain age, go to a specific school, and belong to a particular race), this identity is primarily determined by forces outside the individual. During adolescence individuals must create an identity for themselves. They have to make educational, occupational, marital, and ideological choices that have long-range implications for the rest of their lives. Although identity achievement is frightening because individuals must take full responsibility for their decisions, which may turn out wrong, a meaningful existence is not possible without identity achievement.

Self-enhancement corresponds primarily to Kohlberg's second stage of moral development, instrumental purpose and exchange. Self-enhancement is essentially a selfish activity in which individuals are primarily interested in exploring their own dimensions and creating their own life-styles. However, self-enhancement is also often a social process involving interacting with a variety of different people and playing a variety of different roles. To do this individuals must be able to function at least at Stage 3 (mutual interpersonal expectations, relationships, and interpersonal conformity) and Stage 4 (social system and conscience) and, possibly, Stage 5 (social contract) and Stage 6 (universal ethical principles).

Laing's Study of Schizophrenia

R. D. Laing's (1965) study of schizophrenia provides support for the hypothesis that competence (security) is a prerequisite for self-enhancement. Laing suggests that schizophrenia begins with ontological insecurity. Pre-schizophrenics do not know, from one moment to the next, whether they are going to survive. Laing (1965, p. 42) describes the ontologically insecure individual as follows:

> The (ontologically insecure) individual in the ordinary circumstances of living may feel more unreal than real; in a literal sense, more dead than alive; precariously differentiated from the rest of the world, so that his identity and autonomy are always in question. He may lack the experience of his own temporal continuity. He may not possess an overriding sense of personal consistency or cohesiveness. He may feel more insubstantial than substantial, and unable to assume that the stuff he is made of is genuine, good, valuable. And he may feel his self as partially divorced from his body.

While most people seek pleasure, ontologically insecure individuals seek only survival. While most people are enjoying the dance of life, ontologically insecure individuals are on the sidelines clinging to their chairs.

To deal with ontological insecurity, people withdraw from the world and other people. They spend most of their time alone, reading books in their rooms, taking long walks in the woods, or going for long rides in the country. By withdrawing, they hope to protect themselves from being overwhelmed. In addition to withdrawing physically, they hide psychologically. They create a false self behind which to hide their true self. To accomplish this they separate their mind from their body. They view their true self (mind) as riding around in their body like a man on a horse and then use their body like a puppet to create a false self. They cause their body to act in ways that do not represent their true feelings, beliefs, and emotions. If they find something funny, they cause their body to cry, and if they are sad, they laugh. In this way they protect their true self by preventing others from ever getting near it. Usually the false self is designed in such a manner that it fulfills the expectations (or demands) of others. Thus the false self may be a "good girl" if this is what the child's parents want, or it may be the "stud" if this is what the man's wife wants. The false self is also designed to minimize social difficulties. Ontologically insecure persons are actors and spend hours perfecting the roles they use for protection. They are never spontaneous. Every move they make, every emotion they express, is calculated.

Hiding behind the false self gives ontologically insecure persons a sense of safety and even omnipotence. Their true self peers out from behind the false self and laughs at all the other mortals making fools of themselves by being genuine. At the same time, however, this strategy leaves them lonely, impoverished, and out of touch with reality. They can never honestly relate to others. They can never do what their true self really wants to do because this would expose them. As a result, their true self never has a chance to develop. The only satisfaction it receives is through fantasy, and fantasy grows stale when it is not fired by real experiences. Refusing to test reality and continually spinning fantasies cause them to lose contact with reality. It becomes more and more difficult to differentiate real people from the figures that they have dreamed up. The frustration experienced by the true self at never being able to come out and enjoy the warmth of the real world produces not only depression but also anger against the people who are enjoying life. Laing (1965, p. 91) describes the plight of the preschizophrenic as follows:

> If the patient contrasts his own inner emptiness, worthlessness, coldness, desolation, dryness, with the abundance, worth, warmth, companionship that he may yet believe to be elsewhere (a belief which often grows to fantastically idealized proportions, uncorrected as it is by any direct experience), there is evoked a welter of conflicting emotions, from a desperate longing and yearning for what others have and he lacks, to frantic envy and hatred of all that is theirs and not his, or a desire to destroy all the goodness, freshness, richness in the world. These feelings may, in turn, be offset by counterattitudes of disdain, contempt, disgust, or indifference.

With time, the preschizophrenic's system of defense begins to break down. The true self becomes more and more impoverished. The fantasies become more and more out of control. Though awake, the preschizophrenic begins to live in a dream world. In addition, the true self begins to lose control over the false self. Because of its loss of contact with reality, the true self no longer knows which acting is effective (realistic) and which acting is recognized as phony. As a result, compulsions develop. Individuals find themselves having to do something or be overwhelmed with anxiety. Thus the "nice girl" has to say "thank you" a minimum of ten times each hour and the "stud" has to make a new conquest each week to feel safe.

A crisis takes place at this point, and individuals choose either to destroy the false self and expose the true self to the world, or to retreat further. Choosing the former leads to improved psychological health, while choosing the latter leads to schizophrenia. The latter course involves giving up entirely and seeking a living death. If you are dead, no one can hurt you. They stop trying to control the images inside their head or the compulsive behaviors that make up their false self. They no longer care what other people think. Actual physical death means nothing to them, so they may stop eating. Although this retreat brings temporary relief, it also brings total chaos and, eventually, overwhelming terror.

Laing's study of schizophrenia demonstrates that pervasive insecurity (incompetence) prevents self-enhancement. Ontologically insecure individuals are afraid to expose their true self to other people and real life and, as a result, it is stillborn. It never develops; it never flowers.

Self-Enhancement as Self-Actualization

The two psychologists who have dealt most extensively with self-enhancement are Fritz Perls and Carl Rogers. These psychologists view self-enhancement as the actualization of an inner potential. They talk about "being what you are." The self-enhancement of wheat germ is to become wheat rather than oak trees or sunflowers. Each person is equipped with an inner blueprint or gyroscope, and self-enhancement simply involves actualizing this blueprint or following the gyroscope. The environment can either retard or facilitate the actualization of an inner potential, but it does not alter potential itself. Opposed to Perls and Rogers are psychologists who are less certain about the existence of an inner potential. Among those opposed to Perls and Rogers are learning theorists, psychological anthropologists, Jungians, and existentialists. In discussing self-enhancement, I shall first present the views of Perls and Rogers and then the views of their opponents.

Perls's Concept of Self-Actualization

Perls (1972) felt that the ultimate goal of life is self-actualization, that is, people reaching their potentials. Whenever people try to become something other than their potential, they are in trouble. Although they may succeed in becoming something else, the something else will be false, and their existence will lack vitality.

Perls felt that the arch enemy of self-actualization is society and, in particular, the internalized social rules (conscience, superego) or "shoulds" that society socializes into everyone. Most animals neither live in societies nor are socialized, and as a result they have no difficulty self-actualizing themselves. Baby elephants grow up to be adult elephants and do not aspire to be eagles and fly in the air. Baby eagles grow up to be adult eagles and do not aspire to become elephants and push over trees. With people, however, it is different. People live in societies that put forth social rules and descriptions of ideal citizens. Societies reward people for conforming to the rules and ideals and punish people for deviating from them. Once these rules and ideals have been internalized, individuals reward themselves for obeying the rules and achieving the ideals and are critical of themselves when they deviate from them. As a result of these pressures, people often give up the actualization of their potential in order to live up to the prescriptions of society.

To protect the individual from society, Perls has formulated a set of rules to live by that emphasize the primacy of the individual. The first rule is that each person is in the world to fulfill his or her own potential and not to live up to other people's expectations.

A second rule is that each person is responsible for his or her own happiness, and not for the happiness of others. For example, if someone is in a relationship and is not enjoying it while his or her partner is, that person should break it off. The partner's hurt is not the responsibility of the person. Only a person's own hurt is his or her responsibility. A third rule concerns guilt. This rule states that an individual should never feel guilt for not living up to the expectations of others or violating social or moral standards. Instead this person should transform his or her guilt feelings into feelings of resentment against others' expectations and social and moral rules. Perls illustrates the use of this rule in discussing his own guilt feelings for having left relatives to die in Hitler's Germany:

> I woke up this morning dazed and heavy. Sitting on my bed, numbed and in a trance, as I have seen inmates of mental hospitals withdrawn into their ruminations. Ghosts, Hitler's victims, mostly my and Lore's relations, visiting me, pointing their fingers: "You could have saved me," bent on making me feel guilty and responsible for them.
>
> But I am holding onto my credo: "I am responsible only for myself. You are responsible for yourselves. I resent your demands on me, as I resent any intrusion into my way of being" (Perls, 1972, p. 127).

As you probably have already noted, Perls's rules are all Stage 2 morality (individualism, instrumental purpose, and exchange), and are entirely lacking in altruism or social responsibility.

Perls's (1972) autobiography, *In and Out the Garbage Pail,* shows that Perls lived in a manner consistent with his philosophy. In pursuing his destiny he lived in a variety of places: Germany, South Africa, New York, Miami, Los Angeles, and Big Sur, and visited many more places (for example, Japan and Israel). Although he was a successful psychoanalyst, founded the South African Psychoanalytic Association, and even met Freud, he broke with psychoanalysis to develop his own therapy, gestalt therapy. Throughout his life he developed a wide variety of sexual, social, and professional relationships, many of which he broke when they no longer facilitated the enhancement of his potential. As an example of the nonconventional nature of his social relationships, contrast what he has to say about a lover, Marty, with what he has to say about his wife, Lore. To Marty, Perls (1972, pp. 194-96) wrote the following letter:

> When I met you, you were beautiful beyond description. A straight strong Greek nose, which you later destroyed to get a "pretty" face. When you did

this, when you had your nose baptized, you became a stranger. You had everything in excess—intelligence and vanity, frigidity and passion, cruelty and efficiency, recklessness and depression, promiscuity and loyalty, contempt and enthusiasm.

When I say you *were,* I am not correct. You still *are,* and you are very much alive, though more consolidated. I still love you and you love me, no longer with passion, but with trust and appreciation.

When I look back on our years, what comes up first is not our fierce lovemaking and our even more fierce fights, but your gratefulness: "You gave me back my children."

I found you despondent, nearly suicidal, disappointed in your marriage, chained down by two children, with whom you had lost touch.

I was proud to take you up and to mold you to my and your needs. You loved and admired me as therapist and, at the same time, became my therapist, cutting with your cruel honesty through my phoniness, bullshit and manipulations. Never was so much equal give and take between us as then.

Then came the time when I took you to Europe. Paris, some insane jealousy bouts on my part, some wild orgies, exciting, but not really happy. That happiness came in Italy. I was so proud to show you real beauty, as if I owned it and to help you overcome your mediocre taste in art. Of course we got drunk with Venice and . . .

That Aida performance in Verona! An ancient Roman amphitheater holding twenty—thirty thousand people. The stage? No stage. The one end of the theater built up in giant three-dimensional lifelike props, a slice of Egypt transported from another continent. It is night, nearly dark. Sections of the audience lit with hundreds of candles. Then the performance. Voices floating with gripping intensity over us and through us. The finale: torches flaming into infinite space and dying voices touching eternity.

It was not easy to wake up to the hustle and bustle of the leaving crowd.

The open air opera in Rome was an artifact by comparison, never letting you forget that you are attending a performance.

Our nights. No pressure to go home, no fear of getting too little sleep. Getting the last drop from our experiencing each other. "Tonight was the best" became a stock phrase, but it was true, an ever-increasing intensity of being there for each other. There is no poetry to describe those weeks, only amateurish stutter.

In this life you don't get something for nothing. I had to pay dearly for my happiness. Back in Miami I became more and more possessive. My jealousy reached truly psychotic proportions. Whenever we were separated—and we were most of the day—I got restless, checked up on you, drove several times a day by your house. I could not concentrate on anything except: "Marty, where are you now, with whom are you?"

Until Peter came into our life and you fell in love with him. He did not care much about you. For you, he was a respite from me and my torturing. He was easy-going, an entertaining *raconteur.* It was impossible to be bored in his presence. He was young and beautiful and I was old and vicious. To complicate matters still further: I, too, was, and still am, fond of him.

The heavens caved in for me. I was left with debasing myself on the outside and nursing wild revenge fantasies on the inside.

All attempts to break off with you failed. Then I did something which, looking backwards, appears an attempt to commit suicide without the stigma of such a cowardice.

I survived those operations. I survived our separation. I survived our final fights and reconciliation. I am here and you are there. It feels good and solid whenever we meet again.

> Thank you for being the most important person in my life.

About his wife Perls (1972 p. 264) states:

> I don't feel good writing about Lore. I always feel a mixture of defensiveness and aggressiveness. When Renate, our elder child, was born, I was fond of her and even began to reconcile myself somewhat to being a married man. But when later I was blamed for anything that went wrong, I began to withdraw more and more from my role as a *pater familias.* They both lived, maybe still do, in a very peculiar clutching symbiosis.
>
> Steve, our son, was born in South Africa and was always treated by his sister as a dunce. He developed in the opposite direction. While Renate is a phony, he is real, slow, dependable, rather phobic and stubborn in asking and accepting any support. I was moved when I got last Christmas the first personal and warm letter from him.
>
> We have four grandchildren. No great-grandchildren yet.
>
> Maybe one day I will feel like sorting myself out and will write about my voyeuristic compulsions centered around Lore, about her sometimes brilliant insights and her care for me when I was sick.
>
> Right now it appears to me that we lived essentially parallel to each other, with relatively few peak experiences of violent fights and love, spending much of our talks in tedious "can you beat that" games.*

Perls is almost brutally honest and definitely individualistic.

Rogers's Theory of Self-Actualization

Like Perls, Rogers (1961, 1977) feels that the ultimate goal of life is self-actualization. He believes that every organism possesses a tendency toward growth, construc-

---

*From *In and Out the Garbage Pail,* by Fritz Perls. Copyright © 1969 by Real People Press, Moab, Utah.

tive activity, and actualization. Although the environment may hamper and distort this tendency, it cannot eliminate it, except by killing the organism. Rogers depends on this positive growth tendency in doing therapy with disturbed individuals. Rogers feels that if an atmosphere of concern and safety can be created for neurotic or psychotic individuals, they will solve their own problems.

Like Perls, Rogers is distrustful of socialization. He sees the internalization of social rules, which he calls conditions of worth, as the primary cause of maladjustment and failure to self-actualize. Unlike Perls, however, he does not tend toward the antisocial. He does not advocate the philosophy of everybody for themselves. Instead he sees people as basically good and altruistic. As people self-actualize, they come more and more to care about other people and their actualization.

Let me present Rogers's theory of self-actualization in some detail. According to Rogers, newborn infants have three basic characteristics: they are self-actualizing, guided by organismic values, and congruent. Self-actualization involves actualizing their inner potential. It involves becoming that which they are. It involves developing all of their abilities and experiencing all that life has to offer. In self-actualizing there are some growth experiences in which almost everyone participates, for example, learning to walk and talk, experiencing the beauty of sunrises and sunsets, and falling in love. Beyond these basic growth experiences, however, self-actualization entails experiences that are unique to each individual. Self-actualization for Albert Schweitzer involved writing books of philosophy, restoring and playing organs, and becoming a jungle doctor. For Leo Tolstoy, self-actualization involved writing novels and other books and becoming a pacifist and mystic. For Eleanor Roosevelt, it involved fighting for minority rights and promoting the United Nations.

In achieving self-actualization newborn infants are guided by organismic values, which are biologically based and known through inner feelings. That which feels good is good and that which feels bad is bad. Urinating is good because it feels good to empty a swollen bladder. Wet pants are bad because they cause rashes and give off an offensive odor, that is, because they feel bad. Since people are basically constructive and altruistic, being guided by organismic values does not lead to rape and murder as Freud would predict. Instead being guided by organismic values leads to creative and loving acts.

Congruence involves being open to both inner and outer experience. It involves an absence of defense mechanisms. The picture that people have within their heads of what is going on inside their bodies and in the external world is consistent (congruent) with that which is actually happening inside their bodies and in the external world. Being turned on sexually is not misinterpreted as love, and failing a single test is not used as evidence of brain damage and mental retardation. Congruence also involves an intellectual quickness in which the dance that people have with their environment is sensitive, efficient, and vital.

If infants are given unconditional positive regard, that is, love simply for being what they are, in their entirety, they will continue to self-actualize, to be guided by organismic values, and to be congruent. They will grow up to be healthy, self-actualizing adults. On the other hand, if parents give their children conditional positive regard, that is, love that is contingent upon children behaving in ways consistent with their parents' values, neurosis follows. Since children need love and approval to survive, they are forced to behave in ways consistent with their parents' values, and eventually they internalize these values. Once parental values have been internalized, once they have reached what Rogers calls conditions of worth, children feel a great deal of anxiety and guilt when they do not live up to them. Neurosis is a product of the conflict between organismic values and conditions of worth. People are torn between that which feels right and that which they have been told they should do. This conflict generates anxiety and depression.

If they live in terms of their organismic values, they feel immoral and hate themselves. On the other hand, if they live in terms of the conditions of worth, life is meaningless. It has no vitality. It is passing them by. People experience a great deal of confusion about who they really are. They cannot decide whether they are their organismic values or their conditions of worth. To relieve their distress they try to run away through the use of defense mechanisms. They rationalize their empty lives by stating that they are achieving self-actualization by doing trivial tasks. Although people are born self-actualizing, guided by organismic values, and congruent, conditional positive regard produces conditions of worth, conflict, anxiety and depression, and self-deception.

Learning Theory and Self-Enhancement

As noted in the introduction, although Perls and Rogers believe that self-enhancement involves the actualization of an inner potential, not all psychologists agree with this position. The group that is probably most opposed to this conception of self-enhancement is the learning theorists. Learning theorists see the newborn child as a blank slate to be written upon by experience. This position is probably best expressed by J. B. Watson's (1930) famous dictum:

> Give me a dozen healthy infants, well-formed, and my own specified world to bring them up in and I guarantee to take anyone at random and train him to become any type of specialist I might select—doctor, lawyer, artist, merchant-chief, and, yes, even beggarman and thief, regardless of his talents, penchants, tendencies, abilities, vocations and race of his ancestors (p.104).

For learning theorists socialization is extremely important. They do not see socialization as the foe of self-enhancement. Instead, they see the self as created by socialization. Since the human organism has few inborn instincts, without socialization it would die.

Learning theorists have thoroughly studied the mechanics of socialization. Numerous studies have been made of classical and operant conditioning (Deese and Hulse, 1967), behavior modification (Bandura, 1969), and modeling (Bandura and Walters, 1963). They have devoted little attention, however, to its goals, leaving this to sociology and cultural anthropology. The only exception to this generalization is B. F. Skinner (1972), who suggests that most of the important problems faced by the human species, the possibility of atomic warfare, overpopulation, pollution, depletion of natural resources, and overcrowded cities, are the result of haphazard socialization. To solve these problems, systematic behavior control is needed. He also suggests that we already know enough about operant conditioning to implement this control. Furthermore, we have already empirically determined the direction this control should take. We have empirically determined the nature of the ultimate good. Good things are positive reinforcers: food, water, warmth, love, and things of this nature. Positive reinforcers are events that facilitate individual and social survival; the ultimate good thus consists of individual and societal survival. (Since the newborn child cannot survive apart from others, that is, society, individual and societal survival cannot be separated.) Skinner suggests that we use operant conditioning to facilitate individual and societal survival.

Skinner proposes that a worldwide organization be created to reward individuals and groups for the elimination of atomic weapons, pollution, the waste of natural resources, overpopulation, and urban concentration. Although punishment is the primary form of social control used now, it should not be used in this utopia because it is ineffective. Punishment teaches people how to avoid being punished; it does not teach them to comply with the goal of the punishment. For example, when the speed limit was reduced from seventy to fifty-five miles per hour, people did not reduce their speed. Instead, they bought CB radios and radar detection devices so that they could still speed but avoid getting caught and punished. Skinner's organization would be democratic because a social organization in which the controllers are not also the controlled soon becomes exploitative and not survival-oriented. It would also be experimental because a culture that is not constantly improving itself soon dies. Skinner has faith that a world organization similar to the one that he has proposed will eventually be put into effect as a result of cultural evolution because such a culture is superior to cultures that do not use scientific behavior control.

Skinner believes that the primary reason why we have not already created a utopia based on behavioral principles is because of people's belief in freedom and dignity. Like Perls and Rogers, many people believe that individuals are born with an inner potential and that they should be given total freedom to express this potential. All social control, even that based only on reward (conditional positive regard), not only removes freedom but also is a threat to human well-being and dignity. Since Skinner has found no empirical evidence for an inner potential (beyond the desire to survive), he feels that people who speak of inner potential, freedom, and dignity are deluded. He believes that what people take to be behavior guided by inner potential is really simply behavior produced by hidden social controls or accident.

Although the humanists, Perls and Rogers, and the learning theorist, Skinner, appear to be worlds apart, in many ways they are similar. Both believe that values are organismically based. Skinner talks about survival while Rogers and Perls talk about growth and self-actualization. Both are skeptical of current socialization policies: Skinner sees them as inefficient, while Rogers and Perls view them as detrimental to self-actualization. Both believe in democratic political organizations. Skinner proposes a worldwide democratic political organization employing behavior management techniques; Perls was planning a Gestalt Kibbutz just before his death; and Rogers is deeply involved in person-centered politics. (Although Rogers's early career focused on client-centered psychotherapy, he later expanded his interests and philosophy to include person-centered education and politics (Rogers, 1977). His experiments with person-centered politics have ranged from encounter groups of approximately ten persons to one large group of more than one hundred people. As in his work with individuals, Rogers depends on the positive, actualizating tendencies of the members of his groups to create goals, procedures, structure, and positive change.) When all is said and done, the differences between Skinner, Rogers, and Perls seem to be only a matter of the styles in which they would implement their democracies. Skinner would probably prefer a democracy created by a behaviorist elite for the masses while Rogers and Perls would prefer a grass roots democracy.

Psychological Anthropology and Self-Enhancement

Psychological anthropologists hold a position halfway between that of the humanists and the learning theorists. While believing that the human species has certain basic potentials, like extensive tool use, language, and abstract thought, they feel that it lacks specific instincts. Culture, the accumulated procedures of a given society, must accomplish the function that specific instincts fill in other species. Erikson (1963) has probably articulated this position as well as anyone. On the one hand, he feels that the stages of development that he has laid out are universal; people in all cultures go through them. On the other hand, he feels that each culture determines the specifics of how an individual passes through each stage. Furthermore, the way in which each culture puts its people through the stages is geared to produce individuals who function well in their society and environment. Thus the Sioux practice of producing rage in small children, particularly boys, through harsh weaning creates adults who are particularly fit for hunting and war, the Sioux way of life (or rather, former way of life). Erikson is not as pessimistic about modern Western culture as are some writers. He feels that an individual can complete the various stages of development as successfully in our modern technological societies as in earlier agrarian or hunting and gathering settings.

Carl Jung and Individuation

Carl Jung's (1953a, 1953b, 1957, 1961) conception of self-enhancement was quite different from any of the conceptions discussed so far. Unlike the humanists, learning theorists, or psychological anthropologists, Jung did not deal with the individual potential versus socialization controversy. This was meaningless to him because he believed that culture is, to a large extent, genetically transmitted. Jung believed that the experiences of people are genetically passed down to their children. Each individual is therefore influenced by all the experiences of all of his or her ancestors, and it is in this manner that culture is acquired. For the most part, culture is not something that is forced onto the individual from the outside through socialization; both individual potential and culture are internal. Jung called the repository of inherited experience the collective unconscious and believed that the material deposited in it is topically organized in the same manner that the material of an individual's own experience is organized in memory. Jung called important topic areas archetypes, and he believed that they were composed not only of ideational but also emotional elements. Examples of archetypes include masculinity, femininity, motherhood, evil, animalness, the heroic, and wisdom. The individual is usually affected by the contents of the collective unconscious through visions, dreams, intuitions, and premonitions.

Ego and Persona

In addition to the collective unconscious, Jung felt personality is composed of the ego, persona, personal unconscious, the attitudes of introversion and extraversion, and the functions: thinking, feeling, sensing, and intuiting. Jung's conception of the ego was similar to that of Freud. Jung believed that the ego functions primarily in consciousness and that its primary purpose is to solve problems, eliminate inner conflict, avoid external hazards, and generally insure that the organism survives. The persona is the roles a person plays in society—father, mother, senator, school teacher, alcoholic, entertainer, child, policeman, mental patient, and so forth. The persona is the product of socialization. It is less than the total individual, and Jung felt that whenever people try to be only their persona, maladjustment follows. In this respect Jung is in agreement with Perls and Rogers.

Personal Unconscious

The individual's personal unconscious contains information that has been collected through direct experience. Some of this information is readily available to awareness. For example, although, at this moment, you are probably not thinking of the date when Columbus discovered America, if I ask you to recall it you probably can. Some of this information, however, is not readily available to consciousness because it is too threatening. It has been repressed. For example, our culture severely discourages homosexual feelings, so although most people have such feelings in addition to heterosexual feelings, they repress them from awareness. The material in the personal unconscious is also topically arranged, and Jung called these clusters complexes. Complexes are similar to archetypes except that complexes result from personal experiences while archetypes result from the inherited experiences of one's ancestors.

Introversion-Extraversion

The attitude of introversion involves looking inward and being primarily concerned with inner experiences. It involves moving away from people, to use Horney's theorizing. Introverts spend a great deal of time by themselves contemplating their feelings, human nature, aesthetics, the natural world, and so forth. The attitude of extraversion involves being primarily concerned with events that are taking place in the outside world. It is similar to Horney's adjustment strategies of moving toward and against others. Extraverts enjoy company and activities and are lost when they have to spend time by themselves. Hans Eysenck (1962) has developed a personality test to measure introversion–extraversion. Usually one of the two attitudes is dominant, with the other undeveloped and functioning, for the most part, outside of awareness.

The Four Functions

The four functions, thinking, feeling, sensing, and intuiting, are modes of information selection and processing. Thinking refers to rational, analytic, logical thought. Feeling refers to evaluating, that is, judging whether an event or thing is good or bad. Sensing involves drawing conclusions from sensory experience, while intuiting involves perceiving truth beyond sensory data. Intuiting involves tapping the wisdom of the collective unconscious. Katharine Briggs and Isabel Briggs Myers (1976) have developed a personality inventory that measures the extent to which an individual uses each of these information selection and processing strategies. As with attitudes, one function is usually dominant with the others undeveloped and functioning outside of awareness.

Individuation

Jung's conception of self-enhancement, which he called individuation, involves the complete differentiation and harmonious integration of the various parts of personality. Individuation involves fully developing and harmoniously integrating the ego, persona, personal unconscious, collective unconscious, introverted and extraverted attitudes, and the thinking, feeling, sensing, and intuiting functions. This task is not easy because Jung believed that the personality is fraught with polarities—consciousness versus unconsciousness, introversion versus extraversion, masculinity versus femininity, sensing versus intuiting, thinking versus feeling, and so forth. Large amounts of creativity are needed to develop each end of the polarities, avoid inner conflict, and produce syntheses that allow the individual to enjoy both ends of each polarity. One strategy for working out syntheses involves developing both ends of a polarity and then using whichever end fits a given situation. For example, for the introversion–extraversion polarity people should learn how to appreciate both their inner world of thought and feeling and the external social world. When lonely or bored, they should use their capacity for extraversion to make friends, enjoy parties, and develop involvements in social and political organizations. When overwhelmed by the confusion that often attends social involvement, they should use their capacity for introversion to retreat from others and regenerate themselves by reading, listening to music, and enjoying silence. Jung felt that individuation was best symbolized by the mandala, an Eastern meditation picture composed about a central axis like spokes coming out of the hub of a wheel.

In general, Jung's theory of personality and individuation have not been widely accepted, at least not among psychologists. His beliefs are too far removed from existing data. For example, his belief that experience is genetically transmitted is contrary to almost all of the data on genetic transmission. Recently, however, data are being produced that seem to support his theorizing. As a result, his views may become increasingly popular.

LSD Research

Stanislov Grof's (1976) research with LSD has produced evidence supporting the existence of a collective unconscious. Under the influence of LSD, a number of his patients have reported experiences and produced information about historical periods that they could not have acquired as a result of their own personal experience. For example, one of his patients had the following experiences:

> In the advanced stage of Renata's psycholytic therapy, an unusual and unprecidented sequence of events was observed. Four consecutive LSD sessions consisted almost exclusively of scenes from a particular historical period. She experienced a number of episodes that took place in Prague during the seventeenth century. This time was a crucial period in Czech history; after the disastrous battle of White Mountain in 1621, which marked the beginning of the Thirty Years' war in Europe, the country ceased to exist as an independent kingdom and came under the hegemony of the Habsburg dynasty. In an effort to destroy the feelings of national pride and defeat the forces of resistance, the Habsburgs sent out mercenaries to capture the country's most prominent noblemen. Twenty-seven outstanding members of the nobility were arrested and beheaded at a public execution on a scaffolding erected on the Old Town Square in Prague.
>
> During her historical sessions, Renata had an unusual variety of images and insights concerning the architecture of the experienced period and typical garments and costumes, as well as weapons and various utensils used in everyday life. She was also able to describe many of the complicated relationships existing at that time between the royal family and the vassals. Renata had never specifically studied this historical period, and special books were consulted in order to confirm the reported information. Many of

> her experiences were related to various periods in the life of a young nobleman, one of the twenty-seven members of the nobility beheaded by the Habsburgs. In a dramatic sequence, Renata finally relived with powerful emotions and in considerable detail the actual events of the execution, including this nobleman's terminal anguish and agony. On many occasions, Renata experienced full identification with this individual. She was not quite clear how the historical sequences were related to her present personality and what they meant. Despite her present beliefs and philosophy, she finally concluded that these experiences must have been relivings of events from the life of one of her ancestors (pp. 165–66).

These experiences could only have come from some sort of collective memory bank. While Grof's data support the notion of a collective unconscious, the data do not support the theory of genetic transmission of experience. Many of the experiences reported by Grof's patients were of cultures that were not part of their own ancestry. Grof suggests that all of the experiences of all peoples of all historical periods are available to anyone. All that is necessary is that people stop shielding themselves with ordinary consciousness. Psychedelic drugs, like LSD, break down ordinary consciousness and allow an individual to contact the collective unconscious.

Coan's Research on Individuation

Jung's concept of individuation has recently been supported by the factor analytic work of Richard Coan (1974). Coan sought to find out whether psychological health is uni- or multidimensional, that is, whether psychological health involves the achievement of a single goal or several independent goals. He also sought to find out whether psychological health is composed of one or more Jungian-type polarities. To accomplish this he decided to factor analyze a large number of measures of psychological health. If a single factor were found it would be concluded that psychological health is unidimensional, whereas if more than one factor were found it would be concluded that it is multidimensional. If the measures of health loading on the factor or factors all loaded positively, it would be concluded that a Jungian type of polarity or polarities do not exist. On the other hand, if the measures of health loading on the factor or factors loaded both positively and negatively, it would be concluded that a Jungian type of polarity or polarities does exist. It would be concluded that the pursuit of psychological health is fraught with intrinsic conflict. The pursuit of one form of psychological health means losing another form, unless the individual is exceptional.

Some of the measures Coan included in his factor analysis were measures of value consistency, interest consistency, attitude-belief consistency, self–ideal self discrepancy, physical self–ideal physical self discrepancy, self-insight, experience, early memories, activities, locus of control, reality contact, general beliefs, temporal orientation, and self-concept. Other measures included Barron's Independence of Judgment Scale, the Manifest Anxiety Scale, Rehisch's Rigidity Scale, Barron's Ego Strength Scale, Crutchfield's Independence Scale, the Dogmatism Scale, college entrance exam scores, Consequences (a measure of creativity), Closure Flexibility Test, the Barron-Welsh Art Scale, and Cattell's 16 PF.

Factor analysis produced nineteen factors: Distress Proneness, Objective versus Personal Orientation, Liberalism versus Conservativism, Openness to Experience, Acceptance, Pessimism versus Optimism, Deliberateness versus Spontaneity, Ideational Fluency, Extraversion versus Introversion, General Intelligence, Responsibility, Analytic versus Global Orientation, Organized Simplicity versus Uncontrolled Complexity, Self-Satisfaction versus Self-Dissatisfaction, Scope of Early Memory, Conceptual Elaboration versus Preference for Constancy, Openness to Unreality, Age Stabilization, and Aesthetic versus Practical

Interest. Thus, psychological health is multidimensional. It is possible for an individual to be extremely healthy on one dimension, highly maladjusted on a second, average on a third, and so forth. In addition, some of the factors had both positive and negative loadings, suggesting that some of the dimensions of psychological health form Jungian types of polarities. Measures of openness to experience loaded positively on Distress Proneness, while measures of ego-strength and internal locus of control loaded negatively. In seeking psychological health, most people must choose either openness to experience or control, both of which are desirable alternatives. Masculine characteristics like personal confidence in ability to achieve mastery loaded positively on Objective versus Personal Orientation, while feminine characteristics like social welfare interest loaded negatively. These results confirm Jung's hypothesis that everyone has masculine and feminine characteristics and that the development of both is desirable. Measures of pragmatic control loaded positively on Organized Simplicity versus Uncontrolled Complexity, while measures of delight in complexity loaded negatively. In seeking psychological health, most people must choose between the pragmatic and the artistic, both of which are desirable alternatives. Measures of self-satisfaction loaded positively on Self-Satisfaction versus Self-Dissatisfaction, while acknowledgement of shortcomings loaded negatively. Most individuals have to choose between feeling good about themselves and honesty, both of which are desirable alternatives.

The results of Coan's factor analysis support Jung's concept of individuation. Jung suggested that the various parts of personality, that is, the ego, persona, personal unconscious, collective unconscious, attitudes, and functions, are independent of each other and that all must be developed to achieve psychological health. Coan found that psychological health is indeed multidimensional. The individual must develop a variety of different and independent abilities to be psychologically healthy. Jung suggested that personality is fraught with polarities—masculine versus feminine, conscious versus unconscious, introversion versus extraversion, thinking versus feeling, and sensing versus intuiting. Coan also found that some of the dimensions of psychological health form polarities—control versus openness, masculinity versus femininity, the practical versus the artistic, and high self-esteem versus honesty. The only way in which Coan's work does not support Jung's theorizing is in the content of the dimensions and polarities. For the most part it is not possible to match up Jung's parts of personality with Coan's nineteen factors, though some matching is possible—ego and the Distress Proneness factor, masculinity versus femininity and the Objective versus Personal Orientation factor, introversion versus extraversion and the Extraversion versus Introversion factor, and conscious versus unconscious and the Openness to Experience factor.

Of all the polarities discussed by Jung, the one that has received the most attention is the masculinity-femininity polarity. Until recently, it was believed that an individual was either masculine or feminine and could not be both. For example, the Masculinity-Femininity Scale of the MMPI is put together in such a manner that persons receiving a high masculinity score automatically receive a low femininity score and vice versa. As a result of the women's movement and other factors, however, this notion has been challenged, and it has been suggested that it is possible to be both masculine and feminine, that is, androgynous. It has been suggested that masculinity and femininity are two independent dimensions of personality and that optimal psychological health involves the development of both characteristics. Research carried out by Sandra Bem (1976), using a measure of androgyny that she developed, has generally supported both of these contentions. Here again is support for Jung's conception of self-enhancement.

Existential Psychology and Self-Enhancement

In contrast to the humanists and Jungians who believe that self-enhancement is determined by internal factors, the learning theorists who believe that it is controlled by external factors, and the psychological anthropologists who believe that it is determined by both internal and external factors, existential psychologists do not believe in determinism at all (May, 1958). Existential psychology, which has recently evolved from existential philosophy, holds that human beings have free will and that living involves choosing. Even allowing parents, chance, or circumstances to determine what a person is going to do involves choice. It involves choosing not to choose.

Although the existentialists realize that existence involves certain limits, they do not believe that these limits negate free will. For example, gravity imposes certain limits on human movement. Choosing to fly like Superman will not result in the individual's taking to the sky like a speeding bullet. Yet by recognizing and embracing limits it is possible to transcend them. Respecting gravity and other aspects of the physical world permitted the Wright brothers to build a machine that allowed them to fly. Today it is possible for almost anyone to choose to fly and to actually do so via commercial airlines.

Choosing, and hence living, is a painful process because choices are always arbitrary to some extent. They are always made in partial ignorance. The individual is never totally sure of where each of the alternatives may lead or what they will involve. Thus each choice involves both anxiety and guilt. Anxiety is generated by the unknown and yet-to-be-experienced consequences of the choice taken, and guilt is generated by the possibilities lost in not taking the alternative choices. Choosing not to change reduces anxiety, but it produces large amounts of guilt over missed opportunities. Choosing change produces large amounts of anxiety but little guilt. Regardless of how one chooses, one will always experience one or the other and probably both. Existential psychologists refuse to indulge in the luxury of believing that one has an inner destiny that unfolds automatically, the position of the humanists, or the luxury of believing that one's behavior is determined by outside forces and hence one is not responsible for it, the position of the learning theorists. Human beings stand naked before a complex and terrifying world and must do the best they can, taking full responsibility for all of their mistakes. Given this state of affairs, the existentialists do not believe that happiness is possible. In place of the pursuit of happiness, the existentialists recommend authentic living, that is, making deliberate choices, experiencing the doubt, anxiety, and guilt that accompanies them, and accepting their consequences, both good and bad. Inauthentic living involves avoiding choices, running from doubt, anxiety, and guilt, and blaming others for one's situation. For the existentialist, self-enhancement involves authentic living, making the best of the difficult situation posed by living.

Which Picture of Self-Enhancement Is Most Accurate?

Which picture of self-enhancement is most accurate—that of Erikson, Perls, Rogers, the learning theorists, psychological anthropologists, Jung, or the existentialists? The answer to this question seems to be that there is some truth in all of these positions. Self-enhancement is a creative endeavor and as such it involves a delicate dance between inner feelings and external events. It involves numerous feedback loops of choice, actualization, and evaluation. It is like painting a picture. An artist begins by choosing a subject. This choice is determined by his or her preferences, abilities, and the materials available. The artist then proceeds to materialize this choice by sketching the broad outlines of the painting. Once this is done, she or he evaluates the results to determine whether or not they are beautiful. If the artist likes the results, she or he proceeds by choosing some detail on which to work, actualizing it, and again evaluating the results. If the artist does not like the results, she or he starts over again and chooses another subject, sketches it, and then evaluates the sketch. The artist goes through the choice-actualization-evaluation cycle again and again until the painting is completed. The artist's initial choices involve a lot of freedom and uncertainty. Although almost anything can be painted, the artist is uncertain about the outcome. As the main outlines of the painting are placed down, the artist's freedom of choice is diminished while certainty about the outcome increases. The final painting is a result of the interaction between the artist's inner sense of beauty and the materials available. Each modifies the other. Not only does the artist modify the materials when applying paint to canvas, but also experience with the medium influences the artist's inner sense of the beautiful.

Self-enhancement also involves choice-actualization-evaluation cycles. During adolescence, teenagers make a tentative choice of the kind of life they would like to live. This choice is determined by their inner likes and dislikes, the opportunities available to them, and their own abilities and limitations. Adolescents then proceed to partially actualize this choice. For example, if being educated is part of their choice, they will enroll in college prep courses in high school. Once adolescents have actualized their choice, they evaluate the results. If they find them satisfying, they will choose another aspect of their life-style to actualize. If they do not find the results satisfying, they will choose another life-style and experiment with it. Initially, adolescents have a lot of freedom and experience much uncertainty. As they make and like various choices, however, their freedom and uncertainty decrease. An adolescent contemplating medical school, a life of crime, politics, or subsistency farming has a lot of freedom but little certainty. Once this person has chosen, completed, and enjoyed medical school, however, his or her freedom and uncertainty about the future are greatly reduced because a career in medicine is fairly certain. By the end of adolescence, most individuals have established the broad outlines of a life-style. The remainder of their life is spent working out its implications on a day-to-day basis. A person's life-style is the product of the interaction between inner feelings and the outside world. Each modifies the other. People use the world to satisfy their inner needs, desires, and aspirations, and their experiences with the world modify their needs.

The various theories of self-enhancement, which were reviewed earlier in this chapter, focus on different aspects of the choice-actualization-evaluation cycle. Erikson's theory of identity achievement focuses on choice. He points out that choice plays an extremely important role in identity achievement. The identity of the adult differs from that of the child in that it involves choice.

Perls and Rogers focus on the evaluative aspect of the cycle. They point out the disastrous consequences that result from failing to modify one's life-style so that it is consistent with one's inner values. They seem, however, to have missed the importance of experience in modifying values that were initially purely biological, that is, organismic. As early as 1920 J. B. Watson demonstrated that he could condition a little boy, Albert, who had no natural distaste for rats, to fear them (Watson and Rayner, 1920). To accomplish this, Watson brought a rat to little Albert and then beat on a piece of sheet metal with a hammer every time Albert reached for the rat. Albert was naturally (organismically) afraid of loud noises, and therefore he would double over and cry every time Watson beat the sheet metal. After several experiences with the "noisy" rat, the mere presence of the rat would cause little Albert to cry. As a result of experience, he acquired a deep aversion for rats. By the time an individual reaches adolescence, purely biological (organismic) values probably no longer exist. Even an individual's natural delight in defecation has been modified so that this activity is only enjoyable when it is carried out with the aid of toilet and toilet paper. The negative term, "conditions of worth," should probably only be applied to learned (socialized) values that are detrimental to the individual's overall happiness, not to all learned values. Learning to avoid harmless rats would be a condition of worth, whereas learning to avoid hot stoves would not be.

Learning theorists focus on actualization and evaluation. Operant conditioning is important in explaining actualization. Learning that takes place as a result of reinforcement (reward), such as learning how to dance properly to obtain social approval, is operant conditioning. As noted above, learning theorists have demonstrated the importance of experience in modifying organismic values. The theorists seem to be in error, however, when they suggest that the human organism is infinitely flexible—the notion of the blank slate. Twin studies have shown that heredity plays an important role in determining an individual's intelligence (Newman, Freeman, and Holzinger, 1937; Skodak and Skeels, 1949), potential for schizophrenia (Kallmann, 1946), and even age at death (Kallmann and Sanders, 1948). Genetics also undoubtedly plays an important role in determining an individual's values, though little research, apart from that on sex differences, exists on this topic.

Psychological anthropologists also focus on actualization and evaluation. They have pointed out the importance of culture in determining not only the individual's values but also the ways in which these values are actualized.

Jung focused on actualization. He pointed out the many aspects of personality that can be actualized—persona, ego, personal unconscious, and so forth. He also developed the concept of individuation.

Existential psychologists focus on choice, pointing out both its importance and its difficulty.

The Facilitation of Self-Enhancement

What can be done to facilitate self-enhancement? Carl Rogers (1961) has probably invested more of himself in answering this question than any other psychologist. For child-rearing, he suggests that if children are given unconditional positive regard they will have no difficulty achieving and enhancing a satisfying adult identity. Although the term, "unconditional positive regard," seems to suggest that parents should like every aspect of their children (including their dirty diapers) and seek in all ways possible to satisfy the children's wishes, I do not believe that this is what Rogers meant by the term. Instead, unconditional positive regard seems to refer to a home situation in which the parents love and respect their children as individuals separate from themselves. This situation does not involve total permissiveness. Rules that are binding to both the parents and the children exist, and they are strictly enforced. To give and receive unconditional positive regard, empathy and communication are necessary. Without empathy and communication it is impossible for parents to understand and respect the unique aspects of their children. Without empathy and communication parents are likely to fall into the error of believing that their children are just like themselves. To facilitate communication, Rogers suggested that families hold daily meetings (possibly during dinner) in which members of the family can discuss the things that are most important to them at the time.

Rogers (1977) illustrates the working of unconditional positive regard in the family with a case in which the mother was upset by the fact that the family left their things lying about the house. To deal with this situation she brought it up at the family meeting. After much discussion one of the children suggested that things that were left lying about the house be put into a big box where they would stay for a week. This plan was adopted, and during the next few weeks not only the children but also the parents lost things to the box. One boy even had to go to school for a week in his bedroom slippers because he had lost his shoes to the box. Eventually, however, everyone learned to put things away, and the problem of the messy house was solved.

This kind of child-rearing, that is, child-rearing that involves love, rules, and freedom within the rules, is the kind of child-rearing Erikson recommends for the attainment of autonomy and initiative, prerequisites for identity achievement. It is also advocated by Rank for the development of creative adults. Coopersmith found that this kind of child-rearing produced boys with high self-esteem. And finally, this is the philosophy that is followed at A. S. Neill's (1960) famous (or infamous) school, Summerhill. At Summerhill, no one has to go to school unless he or she wants to. One boy played for thirteen years at Summerhill. Rules are created and modified at Saturday night meetings where everyone, students seven years of age to eighteen, staff, and Neill himself, all have only one vote. Graduates from Summerhill turn out to be as well educated as students attending other English private schools, and they are much happier with themselves.

Rogerian Psychotherapy

For adults who are not self-actualizing because their independent existence was denied as children, Rogers also recommends unconditional positive regard. If these people can find friends who appreciate them for themselves rather than as an extension of their friends or as a means to an end, these persons will come to care about themselves. In the protective atmosphere created by their friends' unconditional positive regard, these persons will begin to explore ways in which they can enjoy life more and enhance their own person to a greater extent. Since there are relatively few people who give unconditional positive regard in ordinary social interactions, many individuals seek Rogerian (client-centered) psychotherapy. Client-centered therapists have put together and enhanced a self that they like and thus are in a position to appreciate the individuality of others. Needing nothing for themselves, they are in a position to care about other people as an end rather than as a means to some personal gain. Rogerian psychotherapists are also trained in empathy and communication skills, and thus they can effectively help clients uncover, construct, and enhance themselves.

Numerous studies have demonstrated that client-centered therapy is effective with neurotics. One of the earliest and best designed was published by Butler and Haigh (1954). It was found in this study that client-centered therapy helped clients move significantly closer toward becoming their ideal selves. Client-centered therapy has not, however, been as successful with schizophrenics (Rogers, 1967). Although it was found that therapy had an effect, causing some schizophrenics to become better and others worse, no average change occurred. The empathic skills of the therapist seemed to be the factor that determined whether the client became better or worse. It may be that client-centered therapy does not work with schizophrenics because they are not ready for self-enhancement. As Laing (1965) has pointed out, the problem of the schizophrenic seems to be one of the basic and pervasive (ontological) insecurity. The kind of therapy needed by the schizophrenic would seem to be one that teaches competence. The success of reality therapy with schizophrenics (Chapter 4) supports this observation.

Perls's Gestalt Therapy

Perls's Gestalt therapy is also a self-enhancement therapy. As noted earlier, Perls felt that self-enhancement involves fulfilling one's potential. Self-enhancement requires no effort because the organism does it automatically. As needs, situational demands, and other incomplete gestalts (patterns) emerge, they command attention, the body responds, and the gestalts are completed. As Perls says, "Don't push the river; it flows by itself." It is possible, however, to retard this process by not being sensitive to what is going on in one's organism and world, that is, by not living in the present. The primary cause of this insensitivity is avoiding threatening unfinished gestalts by shifting awareness from the present to the past or future. For example, a student who has the unpleasant task of writing a term paper may avoid facing it by focusing attention on an upcoming date or by daydreaming about the good old days in kindergarten when playing all day long was possible. When an individual refuses to be aware of the present, this person becomes stuck, and self-actualization stops.

The goal of Gestalt therapy is to help people become aware of the incomplete gestalts they are avoiding so that they can finish them and begin moving again. Two techniques that Perls worked out to accomplish this goal are the topdog-underdog technique and dream work. The topdog-underdog technique is oriented toward helping people become aware of introjected social values (topdog) so that their organismic values (underdog) can deal with (even assimilate) them. In this exercise an individual role-plays the conflict between topdog and underdog, alternating characters, until a resolution is worked out. Perls (1972) uses the topdog-underdog technique on himself several times in *In and Out the Garbage Pail.* The following is an example:

TOPDOG: Stop, Fritz, what are you doing?
UNDERDOG: What do you mean?
TOPDOG: You know very well what I mean. You're drifting from one thing to another. You are starting something like identification, then mention confluence. Now I already see that you are ready to plunge into a discussion on repression.
UNDERDOG: I still don't see your objection.
TOPDOG: You don't see my objection? Man, who the hell can get a clear picture of your therapy?
UNDERDOG: You mean I should take a blackboard and make tables and categorize every term, every opposite neatly?
TOPDOG: That's not a bad idea. You could do that.

UNDERDOG: No, I won't. At least not at this stage. But I tell you what I can do. I can eventually use different typefaces for biographical, philosophical, therapeutic, and poetic material.

TOPDOG: Well, that's at least an idea.

UNDERDOG: So what do you want me to do? Stop letting the river flow? Stop playing my garbage bin game?

TOPDOG: Well, that wouldn't be a bad idea, if you would sit down and discipline yourself like Paul did and write:

1) your biography
2) your theory
3) case histories, dream work, etc.
4) poetry, if you must

UNDERDOG: Go to hell. You know me better. If I try to do something deliberate and under pressure, I get spiteful and go on strike. All my life I have been a drifter . . .

So let me drift and sail the seas
Of hundred verbal oceans
And let such captain be in charge
As is a top controller

So let me sleep as long as I like
And have a lazy breakfast
Then brave a wind that's shivering me
The waves, the boat, and friends
aboard.

So let me travel by myself
Without a wife and children
Without a guru or a friend
And any obligation.

So let me empty all my trunks
Get rid of surplus baggage
Until I'm freed of all that crap
That clutters up my living.

So let me be and die my way
A clearing house for people
A lonely bum who loves to joke
And think and play, and is all there.

So let the world, the cell, the bees
Be filled with thought-emotions
And let me drift and sail the seas
Of hundred verbal oceans.

TOPDOG: I hear your plea
I feel your tears.
Farewell, you lonely sailor.

You made your bed
You forged your chains.
Enjoy your heavy dancing.

Until the last day of your life
When we will part forever.
You married me, and not your wife
And you thought you were clever.

For you is I and I is you
And we will die together*

Perls felt that dreams represent unfinished situations (gestalts) that the individual is avoiding. Dream work involves role-playing the various parts of a dream and thus becoming aware of the incomplete gestalts so that they can be finished.

Logotherapy

The last self-enhancement therapy that I am going to discuss is Victor Frankl's (1973) existential psychotherapy, logotherapy. For Frankl, self-enhancement involves finding meaning in living. With the decline of Christianity and

---

*From *In and Out the Garbage Pail*, pp. 118–20, by Fritz Perls. Copyright © 1969, Real People Press, Moab, Utah.

the secularization of the modern world, this is becoming increasingly difficult. People are coming more and more to believe that the earth and everything on it, including themselves, are only an accident. Atoms came together and accidentally formed molecules. Molecules came together and accidentally formed primitive kinds of life. Single-celled organisms came together and accidentally formed complex kinds of life, including human beings. All of this may be reversed at any moment by an atomic explosion, loss of our sun, or some other cataclysmic event. None of these patterns has any more meaning than the changing designs formed by a kaleidoscope. There is no God behind creation; there is not even any kind of plan. There is no beginning or end goal. There is only endless change coming from nowhere and going nowhere. Since the universe has no meaning it is impossible to find meaning in individual lives. Frankl calls this sense of meaningless and the anxiety, depression, and apathy that result from it "existential neurosis."

To deal with this kind of neurosis, Frankl points out that although it is impossible for human beings to understand the purpose of the universe, it has purpose. Events do not occur at random; they are governed by natural laws. The universe is orderly, and where there is order, there are purpose and meaning. Although it is impossible to fully understand the purpose of the universe, it is possible to catch glimpses of it and govern one's life in terms of these glimpses. When people make the most of each opportunity that becomes available to them, they are conforming to the purpose of the universe, and it is in this manner that they achieve meaning in their own life. When someone does not take full advantage of an opportunity, this person is out of synchronization with the order of the universe and frustration, despair, and feelings of meaninglessness result. Phrased in terms used by other existential psychologists, authentic living is meaningful living, while inauthentic living leads to existential neurosis.

More specifically, Frankl suggests that to find meaning in living people must seek, in every way possible, to actualize creative, experiential, and attitudinal values. Creative values are values that are actualized through engaging in constructive activities. Writing poetry, painting a picture, sewing a dress, and digging a farm pond are all examples of activities that actualize creative values. Experiential values are values that are actualized through aesthetic experiences. Watching a sunrise, listening to good blues, making love, and eating German chocolate cake are all ways of actualizing experiential values. Attitudinal values are values that are actualized by taking a positive attitude toward life no matter what happens. Refusing to be disturbed by a rainy day, a cancelled concert, a headache, or growing old are all ways of actualizing attitudinal values. Attitudinal values can be actualized no matter what happens to people. Even when it is impossible to create or enjoy sensory experiences, people can still maintain a positive attitude. As an example of actualization of attitudinal values, Frankl (1973, pp. 45–46) presents the following case:

> The possibility of realizing in a consistent series and in an almost dramatic manner all three categories of values was open to a patient the last phase of whose life took the following form. A young man lay in the hospital, suffering from an inoperable spinal tumor. He had long since had to abandon his profession; paralysis had handicapped his ability to work. There was for him therefore no longer any chance to realize creative values. But even in this state the realm of experiential values remained open to him. He passed the time in stimulating conversations with other patients—entertaining them also, encouraging and consoling them. He devoted himself to reading good books, and especially to listening to good music on the radio. One day, however, he could no longer bear the pressure of the earphones, and his hands had become so paralyzed that he could no longer hold a book. Now his life took another turn; while before he had

> been compelled to withdraw from creative values to experiential values, he was forced now to make the further retreat to attitudinal values. How else shall we interpret his behavior—for he now set himself the role of adviser to his fellow sufferers, and in every way strove to be an exemplar to them. He bore his own suffering bravely. The day before his death—which he foresaw—he knew that the doctor on duty had been ordered to give him an injection of morphine at night. What did the sick man do? When the doctor came to see him on his afternoon round, the patient asked him to give him the injection in the evening—so that the doctor would not have to interrupt his night's rest just on his account.

One of the beauties of Frankl's therapy is that it is applicable not only to middle-class Americans with health and financial resources, but also to people with whom fate has been particularly harsh—the poor, the ugly, the old, and so forth. Frankl's own experience with imprisonment in a Nazi concentration camp made him extremely sensitive to and capable of dealing with the problems of people who have little going for them in life.

6. Love and Work

Beyond self-enhancement are the values of love and work. Once people have successfully created the major themes of their identity and again have free resources, they invest them in others and their environment through love and work.

The Importance of Love and Work

The two most basic forms of love are probably heterosexual and maternal or paternal love. Heterosexual love involves both selfishness and altruism. In heterosexual love people demand about as much as they give. Sexual pleasure is given but is also requested in return. Heterosexual love is thus an appropriate transition from the self-centeredness of self-enhancement to the other-centeredness of the value stages that follow. Maternal or paternal love is more altruistic and other-centered than heterosexual love because children, while needing a great deal from others, have few resources to use as payment for the satisfaction of these needs.

In terms of the territorial analogy used earlier, once people have successfully developed the self-enhancement belt of territory, they expand the outer boundary of this territory so that it now includes other people (love) and other things (work). They do not give up any of the territory that they have acquired previously, that is, survival, competence, and self-enhancement. At the same time, this increase in territory is not imperialistic. Although people obtain some satisfactions from their spouse and children, they do not view them as possessions, and the spouse and children maintain their own autonomy. People invest in their spouse and children without controlling them.

Maslow's Views on Love and Work

For Maslow's hierarchy of needs, love and work are associated with some aspects of the highest level, self-actualization. Maslow (1970a) suggests that there are two forms of love, deficiency and being love. Deficiency love is a selfish form of love in which the individual is primarily concerned with receiving love from others. Love is sought to fulfill belongingness and esteem needs, that is, deficiency needs. Being love, which is much rarer, is an altruistic form of love in which the individual is primarily concerned with giving love. It involves caring for others simply for being. An example of being love is the love of the father for the prodigal son (Luke 15:11-32). Even though the son had wasted all of his father's money as a profligate in a faraway land, when he returned home his father welcomed him with open arms and killed the fatted calf to celebrate the son's return.

Only self-actualizing individuals are capable of being love. Unlike Perls and Rogers, Maslow did not use the term self-actualization to mean self-enhancement. Instead, he used the term to refer to people who have fulfilled all of their own needs (that is, deficiency needs) and can thus transcend themselves and become interested in others. Maslow originally used the term "good human being" to refer to the self-actualizing individual (Lowry, 1973). Possibly he should have retained this phrase, since it seems to be less misleading than the term "self-actualization." The love talked about in this chapter includes both deficiency and being love. As people grow, however, their deficiency love becomes more and more diluted with being love.

Maslow's (1972) description of the task or calling of the self-actualizing person is an excellent description of self-transcending work. In studying self-actualizing persons, Maslow found that once their deficiency needs had been met they did not cease being active. They did not lounge around all day long; instead, they were highly involved in the performance of a specific task, their calling, so to speak. This calling was not only something that was highly satisfying to the individual but also something that was important to all of humanity. In performing this task the self-actualizing person was simultaneously totally selfish and totally altruistic. In painting a picture, not only does the self-actualizing artist enjoy the product, but so does everyone else who views it. Similarly, in promoting justice, not only does the self-actualizing judge obtain a sense of satisfaction, but everyone also benefits from a better world. Maslow found that these tasks were not performed as ends in themselves but rather as means to attaining metavalues. Although Maslow did not define the formal characteristics of a metavalue, he did provide a partial list of metavalues, which included: truth, goodness, beauty, unity (wholeness), dichotomy transcendence, aliveness (process), uniqueness, perfection, necessity, completion (finality), justice, order, simplicity, richness (totality, comprehensiveness), effortlessness, playfulness, self-sufficiency, and meaningfulness. Maslow believed that metavalues are biologically based and that as such they are universal and can be studied scientifically. Because metavalues are universal, cultures can be judged healthy or unhealthy depending upon how well they facilitate the attainment of metavalues.

Erikson's Intimacy and Generativity Stages

Erikson (1963) deals with love and work in his stages of intimacy and generativity. He suggests that intimacy usually involves a heterosexual relationship in which there is honesty, sharing, mutual responsibility, and commitment. He is very careful to point out that intimacy is not possible without identity achievement. For people who have not fully worked out their own identity, intimacy threatens engulfment. Erikson (1959) states:

> True "engagement" with others is the result and the test of firm self-delineation. Where this is still missing, the young individual, when seeking tentative forms of playful intimacy in friendship and competition, in sex play and love, . . . is apt to experience a peculiar strain, as if such tentative engagement might turn into an interpersonal fusion amounting to loss of identity. (Further) it is only after a reasonable sense of identity has been established that real intimacy with the other sex (or, for that matter, with any other person . . .) is possible (p. 95).

Therefore, if someone discovers that his or her girlfriend or boyfriend does not want to become serious, this person should understand that the distance may not be caused by personal dislike but rather by the girlfriend or boyfriend's not knowing who she or he is.

Jacob Orlofsky, James Marcia, and Ira Lesser (1973) have provided empirical evidence supporting the hypothesis that identity is a prerequisite to the attainment of intimacy. In their study, they interviewed fifty-three junior and senior college men, classified them into one of five identity statuses and one of four intimacy statuses, and then sought to find out whether a positive relationship existed between the two. The five identity statuses included: identity achievement, alienated achievement, moratorium, foreclosure, and identity diffusion. The four intimacy statuses included: intimate, preintimate, stereotyped relationships, and isolate.

Orlofsky and his associates describe the various identity statuses as follows: *Identity achievement* individuals are persons who have achieved an identity by making occupational and ideological choices and being committed to them. In general these people are stable, and their goals are realistic. They are able to cope with sudden changes in the environment because their choices have an internal rather than external basis. *Alienated achievement* individuals have also achieved an identity, however, their identity does not involve conventional occupational and ideological choices. Instead, their identity is based on a rejection of the conventional and an affirmation of intimate involvement with other people. *Moratorium* individuals have not yet achieved an identity; they have not yet made occupational or ideological commitments. They realize, however, that such commitments are desirable and are trying hard to achieve an identity. *Foreclosure* individuals have an identity, but it is not of their own choosing. Instead, it is something which was given to them by their parents or parent surrogates. The individual who unquestioningly takes over the family farm would fit into this category. These individuals do all right as long as their environment does not change. If something should happen to their inherited occupation, however, they would be lost. *Identity diffusion* persons do not have an identity, and they are not looking for one. Instead, they lead either a "playboy" life-style centering around hedonistic pleasure and devoid of commitment or a schizoid life-style—aimless, aloof, drifting, empty.

The four statuses of intimacy were described as follows: The *intimate* individual has several close friends with whom he discusses personal matters. In addition, he has a girlfriend to whom he has made a commitment and with whom he shares both affection and anger. There is a mutually satisfactory sexual relationship, and often he and his girlfriend have lived together for a period of time. The *preintimate* individual has a number of men and women friends. In interacting with them he is open, responsible, and respectful toward their integrity. However, he has not made a commitment to one particular person and, in fact, feels a great deal of ambivalence about commitment. The individual who pursues *stereotyped relationships* has a number of men and women acquaintances with whom he does things, but he is not really close to any of these people. Although he dates women regularly, he views them more or less as sex objects and does not feel any responsibility for them or commitment toward them. The *isolate* has almost no acquaintances; he spends a great deal of time alone. Women threaten him and so he dates little if at all. The possibility of sex is very frightening and, in general, he lacks interpersonal skills.

Supporting the hypothesis that identity achievement is a prerequisite to intimacy, Orlofsky and his associates found that the percentage of subjects achieving preintimacy or intimacy increased significantly as a function of identity status. The percentages were: identity diffusion, zero percent; foreclosure, 18 percent; moratorium, 64 percent; alienated achievement, 88 percent; and identity achievement, 82 percent.

Love for children and work occur in Erikson's generativity stage. During this stage people invest more of their time, energy, and resources into their children and work than into themselves. Their primary concern is the next generation and the future of their society and culture. It may be during this stage that people become concerned with the establishment of their own immortality through their children or some creation that will outlast them—a book, rock and roll song, piece of research, building, or corporation, for example.

Stage Three and Four Morality

The moralities accompanying love and work are Kohlberg's Stage 3 (mutual interpersonal expectations, relationships, and interpersonal conformity) and Stage 4 (social system and conscience) moralities. Before people come to value love and work, their primary concern is their own well-being. Others are used as means to their own ends but never treated as ends in themselves. They have little use for a system of ethics, that is, a set of rules that protects not only their own interests but also the interests of other people. They do whatever they can get away with. Although they may obey laws to avoid punishments and acquire rewards, they do not do so to benefit others. For people like this, obeying social laws is like wearing overshoes in the snow. Overshoes are worn to keep their feet warm and comfortable, not to protect the snow. Their subjective world is a vicious one, "red of tooth and claw." Once, however, people transcend themselves and become interested in love and work, they seek out a system of ethics. Initially, their love includes only their spouse, children, and close friends, and their ethics are concerned only with the happiness and approval of family and close friends (Stage 3 morality). They do whatever is necessary to make themselves, their family, and their friends happy. They have little concern, however, for people who are not family or friends. (This morality is something of a clan morality. No sacrifice is too great for a McCoy, but the only good Hatfield is a dead Hatfield.)

As their love expands still further, they come to care about people whom they have never met. They come to care about the people who make up their society and culture. When this happens, they adopt Stage 4 morality. They support and obey the laws, norms, and values of their society. They like all Americans (meaning citizens of the United States) and insist on supporting the United States government no matter what—America, right or wrong. They appreciate (almost worship) her values—freedom, democracy, individualism, hard work, baseball, and apple pie. They obey her laws and have no mercy for criminals. They believe in law and order, capital punishment, and getting tough with drug addicts, homosexuals, and other derelicts. Their love does not extend beyond the boundaries of their country. They are suspicious of foreigners and their country's enemies are their enemies. They would rather be dead than red, and they have no tolerance for anyone who is critical of their country—America, love her or leave her.

Authoritarianism

Stage 4 morality (social system and conscience) is an authoritarian morality. T. W. Adorno, Else Frenkel-Brunswick, Daniel J. Levinson, and R. Nevitt Sanford (1950) have studied the authoritarian personality extensively. To better explain this stage of moral development, I am going to present their theory and research in some detail. Their research on the authoritarian personality was stimulated by Hitler's Germany, one of the best examples of an authoritarian government in modern times. As a result of the atrocities committed by Nazi Germany, the American Jewish Committee asked Adorno and his associates to study the authoritarian personality so that the rise of authoritarian governments could be prevented in the future.

Using psychoanalytic theory, other people's analyses of authoritarianism, such as Fromm's (1941) *Escape from Freedom,* previous research, and observations of actual behavior, Adorno and his associates theorized that authoritarian individuals are people who have been thoroughly socialized to accept a conventional morality that insists on obedience to authority and rejection of sex and aggression. As a result of these inhibitions, frustration builds up and eventually comes out in the form of hatred for and aggression against appropriate targets, that is, "bad people," people who do not live in terms of conventional moral standards. More specifically, they suggest that the authoritarian personality is composed of nine characteristics: conventionalism, submission, aggression, destruction and cynicism, power and toughness, superstition and stereotypy, anti-intraception, projectivity, and concern with sex.

Conventionalism

Conventionalism refers to the morality followed by the authoritarian. As noted earlier, authoritarian individuals have been thoroughly socialized to accept a conventional morality that insists on obedience and rejection of sex and aggression. Although all authoritarian individuals are conventional, not all conventional people are authoritarian. If people choose conventional morality after experimenting with other moralities and do not accept conventional morality blindly, they are not authoritarian individuals.

Submission to Authority

Submission to authority refers to one aspect of conventional morality. Authoritarian individuals have been taught that they cannot trust their own judgments but must always consult either a superior (for example, boss, father, policeman, or minister) or a written authority (for example, army book of regulations, law book, Bible, or university handbook). Although organizations made up of authoritarian individuals are extremely efficient, they are not very flexible or creative.

Aggression

Aggression refers to the fact that authoritarians have been socialized to hate nonconventional (immoral) behavior on the part of themselves and others. When authoritarians catch themselves or others engaging in taboo behavior, they punish them by aggressing against them. Their aggression is fired to some extent by the frustration generated by their conventional life-style. Continual submission to their father, boss, priest, moral code, and so forth, breeds anger that is displaced onto "immoral" individuals—blacks, homosexuals, Jews, hippies, cowboys, and other so-called criminals.

Destruction and Cynicism

Destruction and cynicism refer to the negative attitude that authoritarians take toward humanity. Authoritarian individuals believe that people are basically evil and that it is necessary to have strict laws to keep them in line. Authoritarians do not like themselves and constantly have to fight temptation. At times, authoritarians use their cynicism to justify aggressing against others: for example, it was easier to send Jews to the gas chambers if it were believed that they were immoral, weak, and corrupt, and it is easier to flunk students if it is believed that they are all lazy cheats.

Power and Toughness

Power and toughness refer to the fact that authoritarians tend to view interpersonal relationships in terms of power. Within the family, the father has power over the wife and the wife, in turn, has power over the children. In the church, the pope has power over the archbishops, the archbishops have power over the bishops, the bishops have power over the priests, and the priests have power over the parishioners. Authoritarian individuals live out their lives highly sensitive to similar hierarchies at work, at school, within their country, and so forth. When two authoritarian strangers meet, one of the first things they determine is their relative positions of power. In addition to this more or less legitimate interest in power, authoritarians have a compensatory interest in power. Because they have been taught to always follow orders, authoritarians do not know how to function when there are no rules. When divested of the props of conventional morality, authority figures, and rule books, they are left very weak. Authoritarians are aware of their weakness, and to compensate for it, they constantly seek ways to prove their toughness.

Superstition and Stereotypy

Superstition and stereotypy refer to the fact that authoritarian individuals have been taught to obey rather than to think. Because they have not been taught to think, they are very susceptible to superstition and stereotyped thinking. Authoritarians are true believers. They cannot tolerate the ambiguity of having to put together their own religion, and as a result, they blindly accept conventional religion. With respect to people, their thinking is stereotyped. They believe that there are two kinds of people in this world, the good and the bad, and that is that.

Anti-Intraception

Anti-intraception refers to authoritarians' distrust of the subjective. Since they already know what is good and bad, they do not have to look inside to find out what to do. In fact, they are afraid to look inside for fear that they will find that they do not really enjoy their conventional lifestyle. To look inside is to invite psychological conflict, and thus they refuse to introspect.

Projectivity

Projectivity refers to the tendency of authoritarians to project their repressed sexual and aggressive tendencies onto others. Because authoritarians do not allow themselves to enjoy sex or aggression, they know little about either and come to hold exaggerated beliefs about how sex and aggression are being enjoyed by "bad" people. They believe, for example, that blacks are superstuds, that hippie chicks scream with delight and have hundreds of orgasms, and that the Hell's Angels engage in fantastic orgies of violence and murder.

Sex

Sex is an obsession for authoritarians. Because sex is bad, authoritarian individuals are allowed to engage in it only with their spouse, at night, in the missionary position, and for the purpose of having children. Consequently, authoritarians do not enjoy sex very much and come to envy the "bad" people who are, supposedly, having all of the fun. At the same time, they condemn these people because they are immoral. Authoritarians' conflicting feelings about sex make it an obsession for them.

The California F Scale

Adorno and his associates used these ideas to construct a personality test, the California F Scale, that was designed to measure authoritarianism. Supporting their theorizing, scores on this scale have been found to correlate positively with anti-Semitism and ethnocentrism (Adorno et al., 1950), political and economic conservativism (Adorno et al., 1950), hostility (Meer, 1959), conformity (Nadler, 1959), obedience (Elms and Milgram, 1966), tendency to judge paintings of nudes pornographic (Eliasberg and Stuart, 1961), and church attendance (Byrne, 1974). Scores on the California F Scale have been found to correlate negatively with intelligence (Jacobson and Rettig, 1959), years of education (Lindgren, 1962), and grade-point average (Davids, 1956).

The theorizing and research that have been carried out on authoritarianism have been, for the most part, negative. To some extent, this is justified. Extreme authoritarianism has produced atrocities like Auschwitz and racism in the United States. To some extent, however, this negativism is not justified. According to Kohlberg, authoritarianism is a stage of moral development that everyone experiences. Authoritarian morality is better than clan morality (Stage 3 morality) or no morality at all (Stages 1 and 2). Authoritarian morality, however, is not as good as Stage 5 or 6 morality.

The Art of Loving

A number of other psychologists have dealt with love and work. They include Fromm, Rogers, Leonard Berkowitz, Freud, and Ellis. In his book, *The Art of Loving,* Fromm (1974) points out that one of the most important problems of the modern world is loneliness. The heterogeneity, complexity, and continual change of the modern world make the establishment and maintenance of relationships extremely difficult. People from different racial, ethnic, and geographical backgrounds often find that they have nothing in common, nothing on which to build a relationship. Social and geographical mobility often end relationships that have been established and make people hesitant about establishing relationships of any depth. The complexity of large cities makes indifference to other people almost necessary for survival. Attending to each and every person encountered in the course of a day in a large city would be overly stimulating. Because the modern world makes loving so difficult, Fromm suggests that we must put forth a special effort to learn to love.

Is Love Being Loved, Falling in Love, or a Social Exchange?

Fromm suggests that most people believe that love involves being loved, falling in love, or a social exchange in which potential mates purchase each other. Being loved involves waiting around for the white knight (or fairy princess) to come along in a white Porsche, sweep you off your feet, and take you to happy-ever-after land. Falling in love is different from being loved. Being loved is somewhat materialistic, while falling in love entails an altered state of consciousness. Falling in love involves waiting to be shot by Cupid's arrows and transported into an eternal intoxication in which people are always happy. Under the influence of Cupid's arrows, time stands still for them and their beloved, and when they touch each other, they touch eternity and nothing matters because nothing aversive can touch them. Love as a social exchange involves less idealism than waiting either for the white knight (fairy princess) or Cupid's arrows. Viewing love as a social exchange is a strategy resorted to after people have waited for the knight or princess or permanent fix (of love) for a long time and are growing old. People then give up waiting to be loved or fall in love and decide to settle for the best mate that they can find given their own exchange value.

Although many people believe that love involves being loved, falling in love, or a social exchange, Fromm points out that these states are not love. Seeking to be loved or to fall in love are ways in which people attempt to avoid facing and solving their own problems. Being unable to succeed on their own, they wait for a white knight or princess to come along and give them a boost. Or they try to escape their troubles through the intoxication of being in love. In the long run, however, running away from their troubles never works. The white knight or princess always has flaws, makes demands, or leaves them, and the intoxication of love is transient. The high associated with being in love results when two lonely people drop the barriers that separate them. Having an opportunity to tell someone else their most intimate secrets and having someone else confide in them is a rare and delightful event. It makes the individuals involved extremely happy. Once all of the barriers have been broken down, however, there is nothing left to reveal. At this point boredom sets in, and the intoxication leaves. Again the individuals are left to face their own inadequacies, and new love affairs become necessary. A social exchange is not love. It is merely a business transaction. It is something that only someone interested in survival, competence, or self-enhancement would do.

Love Is a Skill That Is Learned

Fromm believes that love is an art, a skill that is learned. It is something that flows out of adequacy, not inadequacy. It is a trait that is developed and is, to some extent, independent of love objects, though it cannot be expressed in the absence of others. We thus have loving and nonloving people, not people who are in love and people who are out of love. Love can be developed as easily after marriage as before; this is why arranged marriages worked. Love involves caring, responsibility, respect, and empathy. Caring is an active concern for the life and growth of another. Responsibility involves being the keeper of one's brother, standing by him through good times and bad. Respect prevents responsibility from becoming possessiveness. It involves encouraging the other person to be him- or herself. It is impossible to love someone whom you do not respect. Empathy involves knowing the other person from the inside. Caring, responsibility, and respect are impossible without empathy.

Love is a matter of giving, not receiving. It does not involve keeping track of the expenses put into a relationship and gains received from it so as to make sure that the gains outweigh the expenses. It does not involve becoming angry when one gives a double album for Christmas but only receives a single in return. Yet if a person gives, this giving will stimulate the giving of something in return.

Six Kinds of Love

According to Fromm there are six kinds of love: mother love, father love, brother love, erotic love, self-love, and love for God. Mother love is unconditional; mothers love their children simply for being. Father love is conditional; it must be earned. Mother love instills compassion, while father love instills competence. Both are important. While mother and father love exist between unequals, brother love is between equals. Each gives but also receives. Erotic love is exclusive; it exists only between two people. Immature erotic love is symbiotic in form and involves mutual dependence and loss of freedom. Symbiotic love is not a desirable form of erotic love because the loss of freedom generates a great deal of hostility. Mature erotic love involves a paradox in which two independent people transcend their independence to become a unit. Fromm describes mature love as follows (1974, p. 17):

> In contrast to symbiotic union, mature love is union under the condition of preserving one's integrity, one's individuality. Love is an active power in man; a power which breaks through the walls which separate man from his fellow men, which unites him with

> others; love makes him overcome the sense of isolation and separateness, yet it permits him to be himself, to retain his integrity. In love the paradox occurs that two beings become one and yet remain two.

Mature love does not involve dependency or loss of freedom, and as a result, it does not generate hostility. Mature love also involves an act of will and commitment. Fromm (1974, p. 47) states:

> Love should be essentially an act of will, a decision to commit my life completely to that of one other person. This is, indeed, the rationale behind the idea of the indissolubility of marriage, as it is behind the many forms of traditional marriage in which the two partners never choose each other, but are chosen for each other—and yet are expected to love each other.

Self-love is not the same thing as selfishness. Self-love is a prerequisite to loving others. Jesus asked that we love our neighbors as ourselves, not more than ourselves. Here again we find evidence suggesting that self-enhancement is a precondition to loving. Love for God does not involve feeling affection for a big grandfather with a white beard and thunderbolt in the sky. Rather, it involves loving the values God stands for: truth, beauty, justice, goodness, and so forth. Loving God involves living each day in such a way that the values He stands for are actualized.

Self-Enhancement as Prerequisite to Loving Others

Carl Rogers and Leonard Berkowitz have dealt extensively with the hypothesis that self-enhancement is a prerequisite to love for others. Rogers has found that individuals cannot function as therapists, that is, give unconditional positive regard, unless they can give unconditional positive regard to themselves. He has also found that as clients come to accept themselves, they become more capable of accepting others. Berkowitz (1972) is a social psychologist who has experimented extensively with helping behavior. He has found that one of the most powerful determinants of whether or not people engage in helping behavior is how they feel about themselves. Individuals who feel good about themselves are much more likely to help someone else than individuals who are unhappy with themselves. Various experiments have shown that succeeding at a task, finding a dime, being given a cookie, or scoring well on a personality test all facilitate helping behavior.

Freud and Ellis have also briefly dealt with love and work. When asked the purpose of living Freud responded, "Love and work." Ellis teaches his clients that happiness can never be directly attained. It can only be achieved indirectly as a by-product of love and work.

The Encounter Group

If people are having difficulty transcending themselves and becoming involved in others and the world through love and work, is there anything they can do to help themselves? Although there are not a large number of therapies for persons attempting to achieve these values, at least one does exist. This is the encounter group. An encounter group is a group of people who have come together for the express purpose of getting close to each other, that is, learning how to love and be loved. The encounter group is a recent phenomenon, pioneered on the East Coast by the National Training Laboratories of Bethel Maine and on the West Coast by Esalen Institute. Groups usually consist of approximately ten people and may meet only once, for a weekend, week, or two weeks, or several times spread over a period of months.

Closeness is achieved by establishing and following certain norms. These norms encourage self-disclosure, honesty, giving feedback, working in terms of feelings, giving support, focusing on the immediate present, and being nonjudgmental. The purpose of the leader is to establish these norms and encourage the group members to follow them. At the same time, the leader is also a group member who wants to love and be loved by the other participants.

Elliot Aronson (1976) has provided an excellent analysis of the process by which these norms facilitate closeness (pp. 259-61):

> In the course of the group meeting, one of the members (Sam) looked squarely at another member (Harry) and said, "Harry, I've been listening to you and watching you for a day and a half, and I think you're a phoney." Now, that's quite an accusation. How can Harry respond? Another way of asking the question is: What are Harry's options? He has several: he can (1) agree with Sam; (2) deny the accusation and say that he's not a phoney; (3) say, "Gee, Sam, I'm sorry that you feel that way"; (4) get angry and call Sam some names; or (5) feel sorry for himself and go into a sulk. Taken by themselves, none of these responses is particularly productive. In the "real world," it is unlikely that Sam would have come out with this statement; if he had come out with it, there almost certainly would have been trouble. But doesn't Sam have the right to express this judgment? After all, he's only being open.
>
> This seems to be a dilemma: T-groups encourage openness, but openness can hurt people. The solution to this dilemma is rather simple: It is possible to be open and, at the same time, to express oneself in a manner that causes a minimum of pain. The key rests in the term "feeling": Sam was not expressing a feeling, he was expressing a judgment. As I mentioned previously, openness in a T-group means the open expression of feelings. By "feeling," I mean, specifically, anger or joy, sadness or happiness, annoyance, fear, discomfort, warmth, and the like. . . .
>
> How was this encounter handled in the T-Group? In this situation, the group leader intervened by asking Sam if he had any *feelings* about Harry. In our society, people are not accustomed to expressing feelings. It is not surprising, then, that Sam thought for a

moment and then said, "Well, I *feel* that Harry is a phoney." Of course, this is not a feeling, as defined above. This is an opinion or a judgment expressed in the terminology of feelings. A judgment is nothing more or less than a feeling that is inadequately understood or inadequately expressed. Accordingly, the leader probed further by asking Sam *what* his feelings were. Sam still insisted that he felt that Harry was a phoney. "And what does that do to you?" asked the leader. "It annoys the hell out of me," answered Sam. Here, another member of the group intervened and asked for data: "What kinds of things has Harry done that annoyed you, Sam?" Sam, after several minutes of probing by various members of the group, admitted that he got annoyed whenever Harry showed affection to some of the women in the group. On further probing, it turned out that Sam perceived Harry as being very successful with women. What eventually emerged was that Sam owned up to a feeling of jealousy and envy—that Sam wished that he had Harry's smoothness and success with women. Note that Sam had initially masked this feeling of envy; rather, he had discharged his feelings by expressing disdain, by saying that Harry was a phoney. This kind of expression is ego-protecting: because we live in a competitive society, if Sam had admitted to feeling envious, it would have put him "one down" and put Harry "one up." This would have made Sam vulnerable—that is, it would have made him feel weak in relation to Harry. By expressing disdain, however, Sam succeeded in putting *himself* "one up." Although his behavior was successful as an ego-protecting device, it didn't contribute to Sam's understanding of his own feelings and of the kinds of events that caused those feelings; and it certainly didn't contribute to Sam's understanding of Harry or to Harry's understanding of Sam (or, for that matter, to Harry's understanding of himself). In short, Sam was communicating ineffectively. As an ego-defensive measure, his behavior was adaptive; as a form of communication, it was

> extremely maladaptive. Thus, although it made Sam vulnerable to admit that he envied Harry, it opened the door to communication; eventually, it helped them to understand each other. Moreover, a few other men also admitted that they felt some jealousy about Harry's behavior with women. This was useful information for Harry, in that it enabled him to understand the effects his behavior had on other people.
>
> As we know, Harry has several options: he can continue to behave as he always has, and let other people continue to be jealous and, perhaps, to express their jealousy in terms of hostility; or he can modify his behavior in any one of a number of ways in order to cause other people (and, ultimately, himself) less difficulty. *The decision is his.* Should he decide that his "enviable" behavior is too important to give up, he has still gained enormously from his encounter with Sam in the T-group. Specifically, if a similar situation occurs in the real world, Harry, who now knows the effect his behavior may have on other men, will not be surprised by their responses, will be more understanding, will be less likely to over-react, and so forth.*

The encounter group allows people to experience loving and being loved, and as a result of this experience, they learn how to be more effective with people outside the group. The encounter group also helps individuals learn about and come to accept themselves.

A number of procedures for running groups have been worked out. Carl Rogers (1970) uses a minimum amount of structure in his groups and depends entirely on modeling to establish the norms referred to earlier. Rogers (1970, pp. 47–48) describes his role as follows:

---

*From *The Social Animal,* Second Edition, by Elliot Aronson. W. H. Freeman and Company. Copyright © 1976.

> I listen as carefully, accurately, and sensitively as I am able, to each individual who expresses himself. Whether the utterance is superficial or significant, I *listen.* To me the individual who speaks is worthwhile, worth understanding; consequently *he* is worthwhile for having expressed something. . . .
>
> I . . . am unquestionably much less interested in the details of his quarrel with his wife, or of his difficulties on the job, or his disagreement with what has just been said, than in the meaning these experiences have for him now and the *feelings* they arouse in him. It is to these meanings and feelings that I try to respond.
>
> I wish very much to make the climate psychologically safe for the individual. I want him to feel from the first that if he risks saying something highly personal, or absurd, or hostile, or cynical, there will be at least one person in the circle who respects him enough to hear him clearly and listen to that statement as an authentic expression of himself.
>
> . . . I would like the individual to feel that whatever happens *to* him or *within* him, I will be psychologically very much *with* him in moments of pain or joy, or the combination of the two which is such a frequent mark of growth.

Rogers finds that his groups go through a series of stages in learning to love. The group begins by milling about waiting for Rogers to tell them what to do. As time passes and Rogers does not tell them what to do, they come to realize that they themselves must take charge of the group. Once this is realized there is still resistance to self-disclosure, but this eventually gives way to sharing past feelings. The first immediate feelings to be shared are negative ones. It is safer to express negative than positive feelings. Eventually, however, personally meaningful and positive feelings are expressed, and a healing capacity is developed.

Egan (1970) provides more structure for his groups. He uses a contract to spell out the leader's role, the role of the group member, and the group norms. He has found that this eliminates much of the confusion, frustration, and hostility that otherwise occur in the milling stage.

William Schutz (1969) of Esalen Institute uses even more structure. He uses various exercises to facilitate self-disclosure, giving feedback, caring, and so forth. His book, *Joy,* contains a number of exercises that can be used with groups. The following is an exercise designed to produce affection:

Give-and-Take Affection

When: For most people giving affection and receiving affection are very difficult matters. Many people feel that they are unlovable and that any gestures of affection or liking or admiration are extremely hard for them to accept. If a person "knows" he is unlovable, how can he believe it when someone professes love? For these situations there are methods to help the person experience fully the affection felt for him by others. At the same time the others have the opportunity to experience themselves giving, or being reluctant to give, affection.

How: There are two approaches to this situation, verbal and non-verbal. The non-verbal is usually a more powerful experience but for the best results it should be used after the group has developed close feelings.

The verbal method has been called "strength bombardment." The group members are asked to tell the person who is the focus of their attention all the positive feelings they have about him. He is just to listen. The intensity of the experience may be varied in a number of ways. Probably the simplest procedure is to have the focus leave the circle, put his back to the group and overhear what is said. Or he can be kept in the group and talked to directly. A stronger impact occurs when each person stands in front of the focus, touches him, looks him in the eye, and tells him directly.

The non-verbal give-and-take requires the focus to stand in the center of a circle made up of the other

> members of the group. He is to shut his eyes and the other members are all to approach him and express their positive feelings non-verbally in whatever way they wish. This usually takes the form of hugging, stroking, massaging, lifting, or whatever each person feels. If the situation is timely this procedure almost always develops into tears both for the focus and for some group members. The experience of massive affection is a very unusual one, and the feelings in the participants about expressing affection usually vary widely. For some who can't feel affection to the same degree as the others, the exercise is very disturbing and offers a valuable insight to be developed further. The exercise is concluded by a mutual feeling that it is over. Sometimes discussion is useful, but more often the feelings are so strong that talking dilutes them, and the group prefers not to talk (pp. 195–98).

Are encounter groups effective or are they simply a fad started by the flower people of the 1960s? After reviewing 106 outcome studies on encounter groups, Gibb (1971) concluded that they did enhance "sensitivity, management of feelings, motivation, attitudes about self and others, and interdependence" (Byrne, 1974, p. 300). A word of caution, however, is in order. Encounter groups arouse powerful feelings and emotions, and therefore it is important that they be led by a qualified facilitator. Before enrolling in an encounter group, it would be wise to determine whether its leader is certified. This can be accomplished by writing to the International Association of Applied Social Sciences at 1755 Massachusetts Ave. NW, Washington, D.C. 20036.

7. The Universe

Concern for the entire universe is simply an expansion of love and work values so that people no longer care only about their family, specific career, and culture, but about all of humanity and creation, and the purpose that lies behind (or transcends) their existence. (Some people call this purpose God, though this is not always the case.) This is the greatest extent of value expansion because, in a sense, this expansion is infinite. Not everyone reaches this stage of value expansion because this kind of concern takes a great deal of personal strength and experience. Gandhi's later years exemplify this kind of involvement. As a young man Gandhi was primarily concerned about his family and career as a lawyer. He was married to his wife, Kasturbai, at age thirteen and loved her dearly:

> I must say I was passionately fond of her. Even at school I used to think of her and the thought of nightfall and our subsequent meeting was ever haunting me. Separation was unbearable. I used to keep her awake till late in the night with my idle talk (Gandhi, 1962, p. 10).

To prepare for a career he spent several years in England obtaining a law degree, and then he went to South Africa where he set up a successful law practice. There he bought life insurance to protect his family and sent his excess earnings to his older brother, who was head of the Gandhi family. With time, however, Gandhi's involvement expanded beyond his family and career to fighting the injustices perpetrated against Indian immigrants by the South Africans. Later he returned to India and became involved in the plight of the untouchables and in India's struggle for freedom from Great Britain. Gandhi gave up his insurance policy, stopped sending money to his brother, and turned over his excess earnings to the community instead. Gandhi explained:

> . . . I understood the *Gita* teaching of nonpossession to mean that those who desire salvation should act like a trustee who, though having control over great possessions, regards not an iota of them his own. . . . I then wrote to . . . allow the insurance policy to lapse . . . for I had been convinced that God, who created my wife and children as well as myself, would take care of them. To my brother I wrote explaining that I had given him all that I had saved up to that moment, but, that henceforth he should expect nothing from me, for future savings, if any, would be utilized for the benefit of the community (1962, pp. 61–62).

Eventually, Gandhi gave up his private law practice and spent all of his time involved in satyagraha, the use of nonviolent protest to fight against injustice. He came to see all people as his family and accepted food and shelter from anyone who would give it to him:

> . . . For me patriotism is the same as humanity. I am patriotic because I am human and humane. It is not exclusive. I will not hurt England or Germany to serve India. . . . The law of a patriot is not different from that of the patriarch. And a patriot is so much the less a patriot if he is a lukewarm humanitarian. There is no conflict between private and political law. A noncooperator, for instance, would act exactly in the same

> manner toward his father or brother as he is today acting toward the (British) Government.
>
> . . . He who injures others, is jealous of others, is not fit to live in this world. For the world is at war with him and he has to live in perpetual fear of the world. . . .
>
> . . . If India makes violence her creed and I have survived I would not care to live in India. She will cease to evoke any pride in me. . . . I cling to India like a child to its mother's breast, because I feel she gives me the spiritual nourishment I need. She has the environment that responds to my highest aspiration. When that faith is gone I shall feel like an orphan without hope of ever finding a guardian (Gandhi, 1962, pp. 164–65).

Gandhi was also concerned with the transcendent purpose behind the universe. He stated that all of his activities, including his political involvements, were oriented toward seeing God face to face:

> What I want to achieve—what I have been striving and pining to achieve these thirty years—is self-realization, to see God face to face, to attain Moksha (Salvation—oneness with God and freedom from later incarnations). I live and move and have my being in pursuit of this goal. All that I do by way of speaking and writing, and all my ventures into the political field are directed to this same end.
>
> To see the universal and all-pervading spirit of truth face to face one must be able to love the meanest of creation as oneself. And a man who aspires after that cannot afford to keep out of any field of life. That is why my devotion to truth has drawn me into the field of politics and I can say without the slightest hesitation and yet in all humility, that those who say that religion has nothing to do with politics do not know what religion means (1962, p. 4).

In terms of Maslow's hierarchy of needs, involvement in the universe is comparable to an extreme form of self-actualization, one involving relating to other people almost entirely in terms of being love and acting almost entirely in terms of metavalues (truth, beauty, justice, and so forth). Since being love involves loving an individual for what he or she is, rather than in terms of how this person can be used, being love is a universal kind of love. The self-actualizing person appreciates every individual with whom he or she comes into contact, simply for being. There is no friend versus enemy, in-group versus out-group, or brother versus stranger. There is only humanity. Self-actualizing persons are nonevaluative and "indiscriminate" in their love. They care about everyone.

As noted earlier, metavalues are universal. They represent the ultimate good. Cultures can be judged good or evil in terms of how well they facilitate the attainment of metavalues. By living in terms of metavalues, self-actualizing people are participating in the enhancement of the universe. They are participating in creation.

There is also a mystical or transcendent aspect to self-actualization in that Maslow found that self-actualizing persons tend to have "peak-experiences." During a peak-experience people feel perfectly happy; things cannot get any better. They come to see the ultimate nature of reality; it is though peak-experiences that self-actualizing people have discovered metavalues. Peak-experiences often radically transform people's lives. Maslow describes the peak-experience as follows:

> Practically everything that happens in the peak-experience, naturalistic though they are, could be listed under the headings of religious happenings, or indeed have been in the past considered to be only religious experiences.
>
> 1. For instance, it is quite characteristic in peak-experiences that the whole universe is perceived as an integrated and unified whole. This is not as simple a happening as one might imagine from the bare words themselves. To have a clear perception (rather than a

purely abstract and verbal philosophical acceptance) that the universe is all of a piece and that one has his place in it—one is a part of it, one belongs in it—can be so profound and shaking an experience that it can change the person's character and his Weltanschauung forever after. . . .

2. In the cognition that comes in peak-experiences, characteristically the percept is exclusively and fully attended to. That is, there is tremendous concentration of a kind that does not normally occur. . . .

3. The cognition of being (B-cognition) that occurs in peak-experiences tends to perceive external objects, the world, and individual people as more detached from human concerns. . . .

4. To say this in a different way, perception in the peak-experiences can be relatively ego-transcending, self-forgetful, egoless, unselfish. . . .

5. The peak-experience is felt as a self-validating, self-justifying moment which carries its own intrinsic value with it. . . .

6. Recognizing these experiences as end-experiences rather than as means-experiences makes another point. For one thing, it proves to the experimenter that there are ends in the world, that there are things or objects or experiences to yearn for which are worthwhile in themselves. This in itself is a refutation of the proposition that life and living is meaningless. . . .

7. In the peak-experience there is a very characteristic disorientation in time and space, or even the lack of consciousness of time and space. Phrased positively, this is like experiencing universality and eternity. . . .

8. The world seen in the peak experience is seen only as beautiful, good, desirable, worthwhile, etc. and is never experienced as evil or undesirable. . . .

9. Of course, this is another way of becoming "godlike." The gods who can contemplate and encompass the whole of being and who, therefore, understand it must see it as good, just, inevitable, and must see "evil"

as a product of limited or selfish vision and understanding. . . .

10. Perhaps my most important finding was the discovery of what I am calling B-values (metavalues) or the intrinsic values of Being. . . .

11. B-cognition in the peak-experience is much more passive and receptive, much more humble, than normal perception is. It is much more ready to listen and much more able to hear.

12. In the peak-experience, such emotions as wonder, awe, reverence, humility, surrender, and even worship before the greatness of the experience are often reported. This may go so far as to involve thoughts of death in a peculiar way. Peak experiences can be so wonderful that they can parallel the experience of dying, that is of an eager and happy dying. . . .

13. In peak-experiences, the dichotomies, polarities, and conflicts of life tend to be transcended or resolved. . . .

14. In the peak-experience, there tends to be a loss, even though transient, of fear, anxiety, inhibition, of defense and control, of perplexity, confusion, conflict, of delay and restraint. . . .

15. Peak-experiences sometimes have immediate effects or aftereffects upon the person. Sometimes their aftereffects are so profound and so great as to remind us of the profound religious conversions which forever after changed the person. . . .

16. I have likened the peak-experience in a metaphor to a visit to a personally defined heaven from which the person then returns to earth. . .

17. In peak-experiences, there is a tendency to move more closely to a perfect identity, or uniqueness, or to the idiosyncracy of the person or to his real self, to have become more a real person.

18. The person feels himself more than at other times to be responsible, active, the creative center of his own activities and of his perceptions, more self-determined, more a free agent, with more "free will" than at other times.

19. But it has also been discovered that precisely those persons who have the clearest and strongest identity are exactly the ones who are most able to transcend the ego or the self and to become selfless, who are at least relatively selfless and relatively egoless.

20. The peak-experiencer becomes more loving and more accepting, and so he becomes more spontaneous and honest and innocent.

21. He becomes less an object, less a thing, less a thing of the world living under the laws of the physical world, and he becomes more a psyche, more a person, more subject to the psychological laws, especially the laws of what people have called the "higher life."

22. Because he becomes more unmotivated, that is to say, closer to non-striving, non-needing, non-wishing, he asks less for himself in such moments. He is less selfish. . . .

23. People during and after peak-experiences characteristically feel lucky, fortunate, graced. . . .

24. The dichotomy or polarity between humility and pride tends to be resolved in the peak-experiences and also in self-actualizing persons. Such people resolve the dichotomy between pride and humility by fusing them into a single complex superordinate unity, that is by being proud (in a certain sense) and also humble (in a certain sense). Pride (fused with humility) is not hubris nor is it paranoia; humility (fused with pride) is not masochism.

25. What has been called the "unitive consciousness" is often given in peak-experiences, i.e., a sense of the sacred glimpsed *in* and *through* the particular instance of the momentary, the secular, the wordly.*

Concern for the universe is also dealt with by Erikson in his generativity and ego-integrity stages. If people's generativity extends beyond their own family, career, and cul-

---

*From *Religions, Values, and Peak-Experiences,* pp. 59-68, by A.H. Maslow. Copyright © 1970 by The Viking Press, New York.

ture to involvement in eliminating injustice, disease, pollution, mental illness, and so forth, they are showing concern for the universe. During the stage of ego-integrity people review their life, accept it as complete, and in this manner transcend their finite existence and make their peace with the universe:

> Only in him who in some way has taken care of things and people and has adapted himself to the triumphs and disappointments adherent to being, the originator of others or the generator of products and ideas—only in him may gradually ripen the fruit of these seven stages. I know no better word for it than ego-integrity. Lacking a clear definition, I shall point to a few constituents of this state of mind. It is the ego's accrued assurance of its proclivity for order and meaning. It is a post-narcissistic love of the human ego—not of the self—as an experience which conveys some world order and spiritual sense, no matter how dearly paid for. It is the acceptance of one's one and only life cycle as something that had to be and that, by necessity, permitted of no substitutions: it thus means a new, a different love of one's parents. It is a comradeship with the ordering ways of distant times and different pursuits, as expressed in the simple products and savings of such times and pursuits. Although aware of the relativity of all the various life-styles which have given meaning to human striving, the possessor of integrity is ready to defend the dignity of his own life-style against all physical and economic threats. For he knows that an individual life is the accidental coincidence of but one life cycle with but one segment of history; and that for him all human integrity stands or falls with the one style of integrity of which he partakes. The style of integrity developed by his culture or civilization thus becomes the "patrimony of his soul," the seal of his moral paternity of himself (". . . pero el honor/Es patrimonio del alma": Calderon). In such final consolidation, death loses its sting (1963, p. 268).

The morality of persons who are concerned with the universe corresponds either to Kohlberg's Stage 5 (social contract or utility and individual rights) or Stage 6 (universal ethical principles) morality. As persons become concerned with all of humanity, they give up the ethnocentric morality of Stage 4. They come to realize that their culture is just one among many and that the laws, norms, and mores of their culture are not superior to those of other cultures. They become aware that there is nothing sacred about the rules of their culture and adopt a form of cultural relativism. To provide themselves with a system of ethics, they adopt Stage 5 morality in which laws, norms, and mores are viewed as simply rules that people have put together to make social interaction easier. Laws and governments are viewed as existing to provide the greatest happiness for the greatest number of people and to protect individual rights. Whenever a law or government does not achieve these ends, it should be changed. Different cultures have different rules because they have to deal with different geographical situations and have had different histories. Tolerance and pragmatism are important aspects of Stage 5 morality. It is universal in that it embraces all of humanity in its concern. It does not, however, have any mystical elements. In one respect, however, the morality of Stage 5 is unsatisfactory. It provides little guidance or direction. How do you decide which rules provide the most happiness for the most people? Does the simple fact that a rule exists in a society mean that this rule is maximizing people's happiness? Are not the rules and political systems of some societies superior to those of others? To acquire greater direction individuals often move to Stage 6 morality, which involves universal goods.

Stage 6 morality involves following the "universal principles of justice: the equality of human rights and respect for the dignity of human beings as individual persons" (Kohlberg, 1976, p. 35). Individuals functioning at this stage of moral development obey those laws, norms, and mores that are consistent with the principles of justice but do not obey those that violate these principles. Stage 6 morality is transcendent in that individuals functioning at this stage feel compelled by the nature of the universe to live in terms of justice regardless of the adverse consequences to themselves or their family and friends. As a result of their beliefs in justice, Socrates was asked to drink hemlock, Thoreau was placed in jail, and Martin Luther King, Jr., was assassinated.

Hogan's Theory of Moral Behavior

Robert Hogan (1973) has worked out a theory of moral behavior that is in some ways similar to that of Kohlberg. Hogan suggests that moral behavior, that is, behavior that takes into consideration not only the individual's own wants and needs but also those of other people, is a product of five different factors. These factors include moral knowledge, empathy, socialization, moral judgment, and autonomy.

Moral Knowledge

Moral knowledge refers to the extent to which individuals understand the laws, norms, and values of their culture. Laws, norms, and values exist to facilitate cooperative living; thus, if an individual does not know the rules of a culture it is difficult for this person to cooperate. Not knowing whether it is proper to drive on the left or right side of the road makes it difficult to drive safely. Hogan felt that the best measure of this determinant of moral behavior is the general intelligence test. A certain minimum amount of intelligence is needed to understand the rules of cooperative living. Small children and mentally retarded individuals find it difficult to behave morally because they do not understand the rules. Simply understanding the rules, however, does not guarantee that an individual will follow them.

Empathy

Empathy refers to the extent to which an individual resonates to the feelings of other individuals. It refers to the extent to which an individual feels happy when others are happy, angry when others are angry, sad when others are sad, and so forth. Empathy produces moral behavior because an individual experiencing the wants and needs of another is compelled to do something about them. If an empathic person comes into contact with someone suffering distress, he or she takes on that person's distress and cannot find relief until the other person's pain is gone. Therefore, the empathic person is likely to get aspirin, a psychotherapist, a lawyer, or whatever is necessary to relieve the other person's pain. Hogan has developed a scale to measure an individual's capacity for empathy. In doing research with this scale, Hogan found that empathic individuals tend to be mildly sociopathic, that is, they tend to disregard social rules, laws, and conventions. They find nothing wrong with double parking, not returning library books, sticking their gum on the bottoms of chairs, or smoking marijuana. When the violation of a social rule does not hurt anyone directly and immediately, they can find no reason for following it. At the same time they tend to suffer from excessive role-taking. It is difficult for them to separate and protect their own wants and needs from those of others, and as a result, they tend to be equivocating jellyfish, tumbleweeds blown about by the winds of those with whom they come in contact. They also find it difficult to express hostility, for to hurt someone else is to hurt themselves. With respect to their backgrounds, Hogan found that empathic people tend to have come from homes where they have received a great deal of empathy. He also found that often empathic people had, at some point in their lives, endured injustice, ridicule, betrayal, or persecution. Empathic people know what it means to suffer, and consequently, they want to protect others from it.

Empathy produces moral behavior in face-to-face situations. However, it does not work very well when the other persons are not seen. Empathic moral behavior is similar to Kohlberg's Stage 3 morality (mutual interpersonal expectations, relationships, and interpersonal conformity). Empathy works well when only family and friends are involved but breaks down when country or humanity must be dealt with.

Socialization

Socialization is the process by which an individual internalizes the rules of society, that is, acquires a conscience or superego. Highly socialized individuals are compelled to obey society's rules because disobedience produces tremendous amounts of guilt. Hogan uses Gough's Socialization Scale to measure socialization and has found that, in general, highly socialized individuals are "stuffy, rule-bound, pedantic prigs." With respect to their backgrounds, highly socialized individuals tend to have come from homes where their parents were both warm and nurturant and yet consistently restrictive. Highly socialized persons are similar to Kohlberg's Stage 4 (conscience and social system) persons. Since rule following makes it possible to live in large groups (societies), highly socialized persons function quite effectively within the society in which they were born. If they find themselves in a new culture, however, they usually have difficulty. The rules of the new culture often do not correspond to those of the culture in which they were born, and thus they find it difficult to behave morally under the new circumstances.

Responsibility versus Conscience

Moral judgment refers to the extent to which an individual follows ethics of responsibility versus ethics of conscience. Ethics of responsibility are utilitarian ethics. Laws are seen as means for promoting the general welfare of society, and just laws are those that tend, on the whole, to maximize happiness. Ethics of responsibility are similar to Kohlberg's Stage 5 morality (social contract or utility and individual rights). In contrast, ethics of conscience are ethics based on higher laws that are unrelated to human legislation and can be discovered by intuition and reason. Ethics of conscience are similar to Kohlberg's Stage 6 morality (universal ethical principles).

Hogan has developed the Survey of Ethical Attitudes Scale to determine the extent to which an individual endorses one or the other of these systems of ethics. He has found that individuals who endorse ethics of responsibility tend to believe that people are naturally evil and that laws and institutions are needed to restrain their antisocial impulses. Individuals who endorse ethics of responsibility tend to be reasonable, helpful, dependable, thoughtful, conventional, and resistant to change. Individuals who endorse ethics of conscience believe that people are naturally good and that evil is the product of dehumanizing and oppressive institutions. They tend to be anarchical, independent, innovative, impulsive, opportunistic, irresponsible, and rebellious. Hogan feels that moral maturity involves moderate amounts of both ethics of responsibility and ethics of conscience.

Autonomy

Autonomy refers to the extent to which an individual can resist social pressure in order to behave morally. Hogan suggests that a good measure of autonomy is Barron's Independence of Judgment Scale.

Unlike Kohlberg, who thinks in terms of developmental stages, Hogan believes that the morally mature person has a minimal amount of intelligence, is moderately empathic and socialized, believes in both ethics of responsibility and conscience, and is autonomous. Whether Kohlberg's stage or Hogan's factor approach most accurately represents reality cannot be determined without further research. The value theory being put forth in this book, however, favors Kohlberg's approach.

LSD and Mystical Experiences

As noted several times earlier in this book, valuing the entire universe seems to be accompanied by an element of mysticism. The individual functioning at this level transcends ordinary, fractionated reality and comes to feel a sense of harmony with the whole universe. I do not know whether mystical experiences are unique to persons functioning at this level of involvement; data from research with psychedelic drugs, however, suggest that this is the case.

The person who has researched psychedelic drugs most thoroughly is Stanislav Grof (1976), a Czechoslovakian psychiatrist. He began experimenting with LSD and other psychedelic drugs in 1956, and his early research involved treating neurotics with these drugs. In 1967 he came to the United States, and here his research has centered on the use of drugs to treat addicts, alcoholics, and persons dying of cancer. He has supervised two thousand sessions himself and has records on three thousand more supervised by colleagues. After analyzing these five thousand sessions, Grof concluded that such drugs simply act as catalysts to intensify ordinary psychological processes. Thus, for cancer patients attempting to come to grips with their own forthcoming death, the psychedelic drug simply speeds up and facilitates the process.

Grof also found that there are four levels of psychedelic experiencing: the abstract and aesthetic, psychodynamic, perinatal, and transpersonal. The abstract and aesthetic level involves the intensification of sensory processes. When the eyes are open color contrasts are greater, and when they are closed, the individual often sees geometric designs and architectural patterns. Sounds are intensified, and occasionally the individual "sees" sounds and "hears" sights. The psychodynamic level involves reliving traumatic childhood experiences and acting out childhood wishes. Neurotics experiencing this level often gain the insights necessary to achieve a more adequate adjustment to life. Grof suggests that psychodynamic sesssions accomplish the same ends as psychoanalysis, though in less time, since the psychedelic drug weakens defenses.

Perinatal experiences center around death and rebirth and can often be associated with one of the four stages of biological birth: the intrauterine, contractions, propulsion, and delivery. Each of these stages is accompanied by a unique state of consciousness. The intrauterine stage elicits blissful feelings of cosmic consciousness, while the contractions stage produces experiences of torment and hell. The propulsion stage is accompanied by feelings of titanic struggle, and delivery produces a new sense of blissful, cosmic consciousness. This cosmic consciousness differs from the cosmic consciousness associated with the intrauterine stage, however, in that it is more mature. It is not something that has simply been given to the individual but rather something that has been earned by going through hell. Grof suggests that it is Taoistic in nature and that persons experiencing this kind of cosmic consciousness have a deep appreciation for Maslow's metavalues. Intrauterine cosmic consciousness appears to be similar to the happiness of William James's (1971) once-born individuals, while the cosmic consciousness associated with delivery seems to be similar to that of his twice-born individuals.

The transpersonal level of experiencing involves the expansion or displacement of consciousness so that for individuals awareness is no longer anchored to their physical bodies. An individual may assume the consciousness of another person living or dead, an animal, a single cell (for example, a sperm), plant, or mineral. The transpersonal level of experiencing often involves precognition, clairvoyance, clairaudience, "time travels," and out-of-the-body experiences. Occasionally, individuals have mediumistic and spiritualistic experiences, interact with Jungian archetypes, or experience the supracosmic and metacosmic void. The perinatal and transpersonal levels seem to be mystical in nature.

To achieve each level, individuals must have worked through the previous level. The first psychedelic experience is usually at the abstract and aesthetic level. Only when people tire of this level do they move on to the psychodynamic level. They remain at the psychodynamic level until they have worked through whatever psychological conflicts or problems are bothering them. When they have achieved a relatively good psychological adjustment they move on to the perinatal level. At this level they experience death and rebirth and then move on to the transpersonal. Individuals who are relatively adjusted before taking a psychedelic drug often experience the first two or three levels during the first session. Neurotics, on the other hand, often spend several sessions working with psychodynamic material.

Grof has thus shown that psychedelic drugs do not produce mystical experiences in everyone. Psychedelic drugs produce mystical experiences only in individuals who are psychologically healthy. Generalizing to the value stages being discussed in this book, these data seem to suggest that only individuals who have achieved competence and self-enhancement (that is, worked through the psychodynamic level) are capable of mystical experiences. Only people who value love, work, and the entire universe are capable of mystical experiences.

Working independently of Grof, R. E. L. Masters and Jean Houston (1966) also found four levels of psychedelic experiencing. Their research was based on 206 LSD or mescaline sessions that they had conducted personally and 214 interviews with persons who had taken LSD or mescaline under other circumstances. The four stages that they found are the sensory, recollective-analytic, symbolic, and integrative stages. Their sensory and recollective-analytic stages are identical to Grof's abstract and aesthetic and psychodynamic stages. The symbolic stage involves participating in timeless experiences that have great significance for humanity. Symbolic experiences may involve hunting bison with Cromagnon man, bull-leaping at Knossos, participating in the Tristan and Isolde story, talking with Socrates, or dying with Christ. The integrative level involves a religious or mystical experience in which the individual encounters the "Ground of Being" and, as a result, is transformed. Masters and Houston found that very few people attain the integrative level; only six of the 206 individuals whom they supervised had mystical experiences. To illustrate this level of psychedelic experiencing, I shall describe one of their cases in detail.

This subject was a male in his late thirties, a clinical psychologist who was highly intelligent and had a rich imagination. When he was born he had long silky black hair all over his body, and teeth and a yellow complexion that made him look like an old Chinaman. Everyone expected him to die but he surprised them by surviving. As a young child he felt that he was not like other children; he felt "alien, not really a member of the human race at all, but someone who belonged someplace else and got into this world by accident or under strange circumstances" (Masters and Houston, 1966, p. 269). Although initially he expressed this belief to others, he soon learned not to and instead made believe that he was like other children. He was irresistibly drawn toward evil. When watching movies or playing he always identified with the bad guys. At six he told his parents that he did not believe in God and at twelve he tried, unsuccessfully, to sell his soul to the devil. At thirteen he had his first sexual experience and thereafter was highly promiscuous and experimented with all sorts of aberrations.

In spite of his fascination with evil he always got good grades and eventually entered graduate school in psychology. There he developed an intense anxiety neurosis but managed to deal with the anxiety through self-analysis, self-hypnosis, and relaxation therapy. Eventually he obtained his Ph.D. At twenty-eight he decided that he had a religious problem and tried to break through to "that genuine source of strength and inner peace that men call God." He partially succeeded and felt considerably better.

During the first session the subject progressed rapidly through the sensory and recollective-analytic stages and into the symbolic stage, probably because of his extensive self-analysis. At this level he witnessed the struggle between God and chaos. This experience generated great emotion in the subject and he asked for another session to get at the bottom of this experience. During the second session he felt that God and he were struggling for his soul, that he was asserting his own rebellious will against God. He came to the insight that his fascination with evil was simply rebellion against God.

During the third session he found himself in a subterranean place filled with snakes and dragons. There was no fighting, however, and he felt at peace there. He felt that this was his home and that he had been hurled from this place into the world, like a snarling dog, to cause problems. This origin made him feel more at home with the dregs of humanity than with respectable and successful individuals. At the same time he felt that God was fighting for his soul. At this point the subject looked into a mirror and saw that his reflection was light rather than dark and demonic as it usually was, and he experienced hope. The subject stated that "the hope seems to be a kind of awareness of the possibility of my being delivered from all the punishments I feel I've had to bear for what I never did . . . as if I were to bear the burden of the devil into the world as a little child and then had to live with it" (Masters and Houston, 1966, p. 290). He then found himself in a great hall and felt the presence of God. A lion and tiger fought and the lion won. The subject felt that this meant that his previous nature of blood, lust, anger, and sensuality had been destroyed and replaced by warmth, justice, wisdom, and strength. At this point he asked God if this was all real and God left. He felt great shame for this, told God that he was sorry, and God returned. He rubbed up against God's hand (as the lion) and made peace with honor.

After this session the subject looked younger and felt more mature. The city looked good to him and he felt tranquil, quiet, and happy. During the year that followed his work capacity greatly increased—he saw more patients and wrote a great deal. He also fell in love and married. He felt fully human.

Although the first two stages of Grof are identical to Master and Houston's first two stages, the latter two stages do not match up very well. Yet the perinatal, transpersonal, symbolic, and integral stages all seem to involve similar phenomena. They all involve cosmic and mystical experiences that profoundly change individuals. It may be that there are only three stages, the abstract aesthetic (sensory) stage, psychodynamic (recollective-analytic) stage, and perinatal-transpersonal (symbolic-integrative) stage.

Regardless of how the work of Grof is finally integrated with that of Masters and Houston, the work of the latter researchers provides further support for the notion that mystical experiences are only associated with the final stage of valuing, involvement with the entire universe (and possibly the next to the last stage, love and work). The subject whose case was presented in detail had successfully completed the self-enhancement stage and was well established with regard to his work. He was ready to make his peace with the universe. Furthermore, the fact that only a small number of Masters and Houston's subjects had mystical experiences is consistent with the idea that only a small number of people attain the stage of involvement with the entire universe.

Whether concern for the entire universe produces mystical experiences or mystical experiences produce this kind of concern is an important question, though I do not think that it can be answered at this point. Possibly both occur simultaneously. Only further research can answer this question. Research at the upper value levels, however, is difficult because there are relatively few subjects to study. Even so, this kind of research is greatly needed to facilitate fullest human development.

8. Conclusion

This book contains a lot of words and I fear that the main points that I have been trying to make may have gotten lost in them—a forest lost in trees. To make sure that this does not happen let me briefly summarize the more important points of the book. The bedrock upon which this book is founded is the belief that values can be determined empirically. My argument supporting this belief is that valuing is behavior in the same way that aggressing, loving, maze-running, and so forth, are behavior, and that if the latter can be studied empirically, so can values. Since values are a part of human nature and not supranatural entities like souls or genies, they can be studied empirically. This argument is not unique to me. Skinner, Maslow, Rogers, and a number of other psychologists have also made it.

Given that values can be determined empirically, my next problem was to search the data that psychologists have collected on human behavior and the theories that they have constructed to explain it and try to figure out what these have to say about values. After some thought (and inspiration, I suppose) I realized that values tend to form a developmental sequence of expanding concern. Initially, newborn infants are concerned only with their biological survival. However, as they acquire the skills needed to survive, valuing expands to include competence.

They seek to acquire the skills needed to insure not only their immediate survival but also their long-range survival. Once they have acquired competence, their valuing expands to include self-enhancement. They seek to find out who they are and to work out their own unique life-styles. After self-enhancement has been accomplished their valuing expands to include love and work. They transcend their own selves to become involved in the lives of other people and in causes yielding no immediate benefit to them. After they learn to love and work their valuing expands to embrace the entire universe. They no longer differentiate between that which is theirs and that which is not. Everything is theirs, and in a sense, they belong to everything. Often there is an element of mysticism that accompanies this last stage of valuing.

To some extent this theory is a synthesis of the work of Maslow, Erikson, and Kohlberg. Maslow suggested that motivation is hierarchical in nature. At the bottom of the hierarchy is physiological survival followed by security, belongingness, esteem, and self-actualization. Needs lower in the hierarchy must be satisfied before higher needs can emerge. Erikson suggests that in living individuals pass through eight developmental stages. During each stage individuals must accomplish some task, and they cannot progress to the next stage until the previous task has been successfully completed. His stages are as follows: trust, autonomy, initiative, industry, identity, intimacy, generativity, and ego-integrity. Kohlberg's primary concern is moral development. He suggests that there are six stages of moral development: heteronomous, social exchange, interpersonal relationships, social system, social contract, and universal ethical principles. After examining these theories, I realized that they all had one thing in common: they all suggest that development involves expanding valuing. Maslow's theory suggests that motivation expands from survival to self-actualization; Erikson suggests that development expands from trust to ego-integrity; and

Kohlberg suggests that moral development expands from pure selfishness (heteronomous morality) to universal ethical principles. It is this common theme that I used as the basis of my theory of values. Although in discussing value expansion I wrote about discrete stages, this was simply a literary device to facilitate exposition. Actually, the expansion of concern is continuous like the expanding shore line of a pond as it is filled with water.

Once I had constructed a theory of valuing I devoted a chapter to each stage of value expansion and attempted to present the theory and data relevant to each stage. In the chapter on survival, I discussed Freud's concepts of eros and thanatos, sex, aggression, and death. The chapter on competence is the longest because a great deal of work has been done on this topic. In this chapter I discussed intelligence, the neo-Freudian ego psychologists, ego-strength, internal locus of control, learned helplessness, conformity, need for achievement, behavior modification, assertiveness training, rational-emotive therapy, and reality therapy. In the chapter on self-enhancement I discussed Erikson's ideas concerning identity achievement and the self-enhancement theories of Perls, Rogers, Skinner, cultural anthropology, Jung, and existential psychology. In the chapter on love and work I presented Fromm, Erikson, and Maslow's observations on love, Maslow's theorizing on the work of the self-actualizing individual, some of the theory and research on authoritarianism, and a discussion of encounter groups. In the last chapter, the chapter on the universe, I discussed being love, peak-experiences, Hogan's theory of moral behavior, and the research of Grof and of Masters and Houston on LSD-facilitated mystical experiences.

After having worked out this theory of valuing, I have found that it has been useful to me in a number of ways. Most importantly, it has given me some insight into the nature of values. When I was a freshman in college I read a few works on philosophical naturalism and concluded that there was no moral order in the universe. I believed that the world and we who inhabited it were all accidents and it did not matter what we did. I also believed that random motion was random motion whether it took the form of a winning number on a roulette wheel or the crucifixion of Jesus Christ. My theory of values has converted me from this position. I now believe that the universe is not chaotic, but extremely orderly, and it is out of this order that moral order (values) also comes. From the evidence available at present, this order seems to take the form of expanding valuing, though new data will undoubtedly modify the picture.

This theory has also provided me with a framework for fitting together such divergent bodies of theory and data as Freud's psychoanalysis, learned helplessness, Maslow's theory of personality, Grof's research with LSD, and so on. During high school, college, graduate school, and my teaching career I have been absorbing many diverse psychologies, hoping that eventually they would all fall together. The synthesis that I have put together in this book is probably the closest that I shall come to this goal. I hope that it may also be of some value to you.

In addition, I find that this theory provides a new way of viewing maladjustment and psychotherapy. It suggests that maladjustment consists of the inability to expand one's sphere of valuing. Maladjustment involves being stuck. Depending upon where the individual is stuck, different therapies are called for. For individuals who have failed competence, assertiveness training, behavior modification, rational-emotive therapy, or reality therapy should be used. For self-enhancement problems Rogerian, client-centered therapy, or Gestalt therapy should be used. For problems with love, encounter groups are effective, and LSD therapy may facilitate the achievement of relatedness to the universe.

This theory also effectively deals with the want versus should dilemma. In general, people believe that some values are higher or better (the shoulds) than others (the wants). Furthermore, some individuals believe that lower and higher values will always be in conflict. Thus St. Paul complains that that which he would do, he does not, and that which he would not do, he does. And Freud suggests that conflict between id and superego is inevitable and unresolvable. This theory, however, suggests that this is not the case. It suggests that higher values are attained by pursuing lower ones. By doing what they want individuals eventually end up doing what they should.

Finally, this theory is useful in decision making. Although it is not very prescriptive in nature—suggesting that people should simply do what they want to do—it does provide a chart or map that people can use to gauge their current stage of valuing and anticipate the next stage. Knowing where you are going prevents entering many dead ends. It may also give greater strength to values previously ignored by the individual. I found this to be true in my case. For many years I was skeptical of the utility of marriage—more people getting divorced than married in some parts of California, and so forth. Realizing that loving and marriage (meaning mutual commitment) are an inevitable part of human value expansion has removed my skepticism to a considerable degree. I am much more open to marriage than I was before. Though marriage may be difficult, particularly in the twentieth century, it will always be highly rewarding, for human nature demands it for health and growth.

References

Abelson, H., Cohen, R., Heaton, E., and Suder, C. National survey of public attitudes toward and experience with erotic materials. In *Technical Report of the Commission on Obscenity and Pornography*. Vol. 6. Washington, D.C.: Government Printing Office, 1971.

Adorno, T. W., Frenkel-Brunswick, E., Levinson, D. J., and Sanford, R. N. *The Authoritarian Personality*. New York: Harper, 1950.

Alberti, R. E., and Emmons, M. L. *Your Perfect Right*. San Luis Obispo, Calif.: Impact, 1974.

Andrews, J. D. W. The achievement motive and advancement in two types of organizations. *Journal of Personality and Social Psychology*. 1967, *6*, 163–68.

Angyal, A. *Foundations for a Science of Personality*. New York: Commonwealth Fund, 1941.

Aronson, E. *The Social Animal*. 2nd ed. San Francisco: Freeman, 1976.

Asch, S. E. Effects of group pressure on the modification and distortion of judgments. In H. Geutzkow (ed.), *Groups, Leadership, and Men*. Pittsburgh: Carnegie, 1951.

Asch, S. E. Studies of independence and submission to group pressure: A minority of one against a unanimous majority. *Psychological Monographs*, 1956, *70* (Whole No. 416).

Bach, G. R., and Goldberg, H. *Creative Aggression: The Art of Assertive Living*. New York: Avon, 1975.

Bandura, A. *Principles of Behavior Modification.* New York: Holt, Rinehart, and Winston, 1969.

Bandura, A., and Walters, R. *Social Learning and Personality Development.* New York: Holt, Rinehart, and Winston, 1963.

Barker, R., Dembo, T., and Lewin, K. Frustration and regression: An experiment with young children. *University of Iowa Studies in Child Welfare,* 1941, *18,* 1–314.

Barocas, R., and Karoly, P. The effects of physical appearance on social responsiveness. Paper presented at the meeting of the Eastern Psychological Association, New York City, 1971.

Baron, R. A. Effects of exposure to erotic and non-erotic stimuli on subsequent aggression. Paper presented at the meeting of the Midwestern Psychological Association, Cleveland, 1972.

Baron, R. A., and Ball, R. L. The aggression-inhibiting influence of non-hostile humor. *Journal of Experimental Social Psychology,* 1974, *10,* 23–33.

Barron, F. *Creativity and Personal Freedom.* Princeton: Van Nostrand, 1968.

Bem, S. Probing the promise of androgyny. In A. G. Kaplan and J. P. Bean (eds.), *Beyond Sex-Role Stereotypes: Readings Toward a Psychology of Androgyny.* Boston: Little, Brown, 1976.

Bendig, A. W. Predictive and postdictive validity of need achievement measures. *Journal of Educational Research,* 1958, *52,* 119–20.

Berkowitz, L. Social norms, feelings, and other factors affecting helping and altruism. In L. Berkowitz (ed.), *Advances in Experimental Social Psychology.* Vol. 6. New York: Academic Press, 1972.

Bettelheim, B. Individual and mass behavior in extreme situations. *Journal of Abnormal and Social Psychology,* 1943, *38,* 417–52.

Briggs, K. C., and Myers, I. B. Myers-Briggs type indicator. Palo Alto: Consulting Psychologists Press, 1976.

Burgess, E. P. The modification of depressive behaviors. In R. D. Rubin and C. M. Franks (eds.), *Advances in Behavior Therapy.* New York: Academic Press, 1968.

Burks, B. C., Jensen, D. W., and Terman, L. M. *The Promise of Youth: Follow-up Studies of a Thousand Gifted Children.* Vol. 3 of

Genetic Studies of Genius, Terman, L. M. (ed.), Palo Alto: Stanford University Press, 1930.

Burris, R. W. The effect of counseling on achievement motivation. Unpublished doctoral dissertation, Indiana University, 1958.

Butler, J. M., and Haigh, G. V. Changes in the relation between self-concepts and ideal concepts consequent upon client-centered counseling. In C. R. Rogers and R. F. Dymond (eds.), *Psychotherapy and Personality Change.* Chicago: University of Chicago Press, 1954.

Butler, R. A. Discrimination learning by rhesus monkeys to visual exploration motivation. *Journal of Comparative and Physiological Psychology,* 1953, *46,* 95–98.

Byrne, D. *An Introduction to Personality.* 2nd ed. Englewood Cliffs, N. J.: Prentice-Hall, 1974.

Byrne, D., and Lamberth, J. The effect of erotic stimuli on sexual arousal, evaluative responses, and subsequent behavior. In *Technical Report of the Commission on Obscenity and Pornography.* Vol. 8. Washington, D.C.: Government Printing Office, 1971.

Camus, A. *The Myth of Sisyphus and Other Essays.* New York: Knopf, 1955.

Carey, R. C. Living until death: A program of service and research for the terminally ill. In E. Kubler-Ross (ed.), *Death: The Final Stage of Growth.* Englewood Cliffs, N. J.: Prentice-Hall, 1975.

Charles, D. C., and Pritchard, S. A. Differential development of intelligence in the college years. *Journal of Genetic Psychology,* 1959, *95,* 41–44.

Clinard, M. B. *Sociology of Deviant Behavior.* 2nd ed. New York: Holt, Rinehart, and Winston, 1963.

Coan, R. W. *The Optimal Personality: An Empirical and Theoretical Analysis.* New York: Columbia University Press, 1974.

Cofer, C. N., and Appley, M. H. *Motivation: Theory and Research.* New York: Wiley, 1964.

Coleman, J. C. *Abnormal Psychology and Modern Life.* 2nd ed. Chicago: Scott, Foresman, 1956.

Coopersmith, S. *The Antecendents of Self-Esteem.* San Francisco: Freeman, 1967.

Cortes, J. B. The achievement motive in the Spanish economy between the 13th and 18th centuries. *Economic Development and Cultural Change,* 1960, *9,* 144–63.

Costanzo, P. R., and Shaw, M. E. Conformity as a function of age level. *Child Development,* 1966, *37,* 967–75.

Davids, A. The influence of ego-involvement on relations between authoritarianism and intolerance of ambiguity. *Journal of Consulting Psychology,* 1956, *20,* 179–84.

Davidson, S. *Loose Change.* New York: Doubleday, 1977.

de Charms, R., and Moeller, G. H. Values expressed in American children's readers: 1800–1950. *Journal of Abnormal and Social Psychology,* 1962, *64,* 135–42.

Deese, J., and Hulse, S. H. *The Psychology of Learning.* 3rd ed. New York: McGraw-Hill, 1967.

Deutsch, M., and Gerard, H. G. A study of normative and informational social influence upon individual judgment. *Journal of Abnormal and Social Psychology,* 1955, *51,* 629–36.

DiGiuseppe, R.A., and Miller, N. J. A review of outcome studies on Rational-Emotive therapy. In A. Ellis and R. Grieger (eds.), *Handbook of Rational-Emotive Therapy.* New York: Springer, 1977.

Dweck, C. S. The role of expectations and attributions in the alleviation of learned helplessness. Unpublished doctoral dissertation, Yale University, 1972.

Edmiston, S. Murder, New York style: A crime of class. *New Yorker,* 1970, *3,* 29–35.

Egan, G. *Encounter: Group Processes for Interpersonal Growth.* Monterey, Calif.: Brooks/Cole, 1970.

Elder, G. H., Jr. Appearance and education in marriage mobility. *American Sociological Review,* 1969, *34,* 519–33.

Eliasberg, W. G., and Stuart, I. R. Authoritarian personality and the obscenity threshold. *Journal of Social Psychology,* 1961, *55,* 143–51.

Ellis, A. *Humanistic psychotherapy: The Rational-Emotive Approach.* New York: Julian, 1973.

Ellis, A. The basic clinical theory of Rational-Emotive therapy. In A. Ellis and R. Grieger (eds.), *Handbook of Rational-Emotive Therapy.* New York: Springer, 1977.

Elms, A. C., and Milgram, S. Personality characteristics associated with obedience and defiance toward authoritative command. *Journal of Experimental Research in Personality,* 1966, *1,* 282-89.

Erikson, E. H. Identity and the life cycle. *Psychological Issues,* 1959, *1,* no. 1, Monograph No. 1.

Erikson, E. H. *Child and Society.* 2nd ed. New York: Norton, 1963.

Erikson, E. H. *Identity: Youth and Crisis.* New York: Norton, 1968.

Eron, L. D., Lefkowitz, M. M., Huesmann, L. R., and Walder, L. O. Does television violence cause aggression? *American Psychologist,* 1972, *27,* 253–63.

Eysenck, H. *Maudsley personality inventory.* San Diego: Educational and Industrial Testing Service, 1962.

Ferrari, N. A. Institutionalization and attitude change in an aged population: A field study and dissidence theory. Unpublished doctoral dissertation, Western Reserve University, 1962.

Feshback, S. The drive-reducing function of fantasy behavior. *Journal of Abnormal and Social Psychology,* 1955, *50,* 3–12.

Fodor, E. M. Delinquency and susceptibility to social influence among adolescents as a function of moral development. *Journal of Social Psychology,* 1972, *86,* 257-60.

Frandsen, A. N. The Wechsler-Bellevue intelligence scale and high school achievement. *Journal of Applied Psychology,* 1950, *34,* 406–11.

Frank, J. D. Nature and functions of belief systems: Humanism and transcendental religion. *American Psychologist,* 1977, *32,* 555–59.

Frankl, V. E. *The Doctor and the Soul.* New York: Vintage, 1973.

Freud, S. *New Introductory Lectures on Psychoanalysis.* New York: Norton, 1933.

Freud, S. *Beyond the Pleasure Principle.* New York: Norton, 1961a.

Freud, S. *The Future of an Illusion.* New York: Norton, 1961b.

Fromm, E. *Escape from Freedom.* New York: Holt, Rinehart, and Winston, 1941.

Fromm, E. *The Art of Loving.* New York: Perennial Library, 1974.

Fryer, D. Occupational intelligence standards. *School and Society,* 1922, *16,* 273-77.

Gaebelein, J., and Taylor, S. P. The effects of competition and attack on physical aggression. *Psychonomic Science,* 1971, *24,* 65–67.

Gandhi, M. K. In L. Fischer (ed.), *The Essential Gandhi: An Anthology.* New York: Vintage, 1962.

Gibb, J. R. The effects of human relations training. In A. E. Bergin and S. L. Garfield (eds.), Handbook of psychotherapy and behavior change. New York: Wiley, 1971.

Gilmartin, B. G. Jealousy among the swingers. In G. Clanton and L. G. Smith (eds.), *Jealousy.* Englewood Cliffs, N.J.: Prentice-Hall, 1977.

Glass, D. C., and Singer, J.E. *Urban Stress: Experiments on Noise and Social Stressors.* New York: Academic Press, 1972.

Glasser, W. *Reality Therapy: A New Approach to Psychiatry.* New York: Harper & Row, 1975.

Goldfarb, W. Effects of psychological deprivation in infancy and subsequent stimulation. *American Journal of Psychiatry,* 1945, *102,* 18–33.

Goranson, R. Observed violence and aggressive behavior: The effects of negative outcomes to the observed violence. Unpublished doctoral dissertation, University of Wisconsin, 1969.

Gordon, H. *Mental and Scholastic Tests Among Retarded Children.* Educational pamphlet No. 44. London: Board of Education, 1923.

Gottesman, I. I. Heritability of personality: A demonstration. *Psychological Monographs,* 1963, *77,* no. 9 (Whole No. 572).

Greenwell, J., and Dengerink, H. A. The role of perceived vs. actual attack in human physical aggression. Paper presented at the meeting of the Midwestern Psychological Association, Detroit, 1971.

Grof, S. *Realms of the Human Unconscious: Observations from LSD Research.* New York: Dutton, 1976.

Haan, N., Smith, M. B., and Block, J. Moral reasoning of young adults: Political-social behavior, family background, and personality correlates. *Journal of Personality and Social Psychology,* 1968, *10,* 183–201.

Harlow, H. F., Harlow, M. K., and Myer, D. R. Learning motivated by a manipulation drive. *Journal of Experimental Psychology,* 1950, *40,* 228–34.

Harrell, R. F., Woodyard, E., and Gates, A. I. *The Effect of Mothers' Diets on the Intelligence of Offspring.* New York:

Bureau of Publications, Teachers College, Columbia University, 1955.

Hiler, E. W. Wechsler-Bellevue intelligence as a predictor of continuation in psychotherapy. *Journal of Clinical Psychology,* 1958, *14,* 192–94.

Hiroto, D. S. Locus of control and learned helplessness. *Journal of Experimental Psychology,* 1974, *102,* 187–93.

Hogan, R. Moral conduct and moral character: A psychological perspective. *Psychological Bulletin,* 1973, *79,* 217–32.

Hokanson, J. E. Psychophysical evaluation of the catharsis hypothesis. In E. I. Megargee and J. E. Hokanson (eds.), *The Dynamics of Aggression.* New York: Harper and Row, 1970.

Hokanson, J. E., and Burgess, M. The effects of three types of aggression on vascular processes. *Journal of Abnormal and Social Psychology,* 1962, *64,* 446–49.

Hokanson, J. E., Burgess, M., and Cohen, M. F. Effects of displaced aggression on systolic blood pressure. *Journal of Abnormal and Social Psychology,* 1963, *67,* 214–18.

Hokanson, J. E., and Edelman, R. Effects of three social responses on vascular processes. *Journal of Personality and Social Psychology,* 1966, *3,* 442–47.

Hokanson, J. E., and Shelter, S. The effect of overt aggression on physiological arousal. *Journal of Abnormal and Social Psychology.* 1961, *63,* 446–48.

Hokanson, J. E., Willers, K. R., and Koropsak, E. The modification of autonomic responses during aggressive interchange. *Journal of Personality,* 1968, *36,* 386–404.

Holmes, S. J., and Hatch, C. E. Personal appearance as related to scholastic records and marriage selection in college women. *Human Biology,* 1938, *10,* 63–76.

Horner, M. Sex differences in achievement motivation and performance in competitive and noncompetitive situations. Unpublished doctoral dissertation, University of Michigan, 1968.

Horney, K. *New Ways in Psychoanalysis.* New York: Norton, 1939.

Hugo, V. *The Hunchback of Notre Dame.* New York: New American Library, 1965.

Hunt, M. *Sexual Behavior in the 1970s.* New York: Dell, 1975.

Jacobson, F. N., and Rettig, S. Authoritarianism and intelligence. *Journal of Social Psychology,* 1959, *50,* 213–19.

James, W. *The Varieties of Religious Experience.* New York: Macmillan, 1961.

Jung, C. G. The psychology of the unconscious. In *Collected Works.* Vol 7. Princeton: Princeton University Press, 1953a.

Jung, C. G. The relations between the ego and the unconscious. In *Collected Works.* Vol. 7. Princeton: Princeton University Press, 1953b.

Jung, C. G. The archetypes and the collective unconscious. In *Collected Works.* Vol. 9. Princeton: Princeton University Press, 1959.

Jung, C. G. The structure and dynamics of the psyche. In *Collected Works.* Vol. 8. Princeton: Princeton University Press, 1960.

Kaats, C. R., and Davis, K. E. The dynamics of sexual behavior of college students. *Journal of Marriage and the Family,* 1970, *32,* 390–99.

Kallmann, F. J. The genetic theory of schizophrenia. *American Journal of Psychiatry,* 1946, *103,* 309–22.

Kallmann, F. J. and Sanders, G. Twin studies on aging and longevity. *Journal of Heredity,* 1948, *39,* 349–57.

Kanin, E. Reference groups and sex conduct norm violations. *The Sociological Quarterly,* 1967, *8,* 495–504.

Kinsey, A. C., Pomeroy, W. B., and Martin, C. E. *Sexual Behavior in the Human Male.* Philadelphia: Saunders, 1948.

Kinsey, A. C., Pomeroy, W. B., Martin, C. E., and Gebhard, P. H. *Sexual Behavior in the Human Female.* Philadelphia: Saunders, 1953.

Kirk, S. A. *Early Education of the Mentally Retarded.* Urbana: University of Illinois Press, 1958.

Kohlberg, L. The development of modes of moral thinking and choice in the years ten to sixteen. Unpublished doctoral dissertation, University of Chicago, 1958.

Kohlberg, L. The development of children's orientations toward a moral order: I. Sequence in the development of moral thought. *Vita Humana,* 1963, *6,* 11–33.

Kohlberg, L. The child as a moral philosopher. *Psychology Today,* 1968, *2,* 25–30.

Kohlberg, L. Moral stages and moralization: The cognitive-developmental approach. In T. Lickona (ed.), *Moral Development and Behavior: Theory, Research, and Social Issues.* New York: Holt, Rinehart, and Winston, 1976.

Krebs, A. M. Two determinants of conformity: Age of independence training and n Achievement. *Journal of Abnormal and Social Psychology,* 1958, *56,* 130–31.

Kübler-Ross, E. *On Death and Dying.* New York: Macmillan, 1970.

Kurtzman, J., and Gordon, P. *No More Dying.* New York: Dell, 1977.

Kutschinsky, B. The effect of pornography: A pilot experiment on perception, behavior, and attitudes. In *Technical Report of the Commission on Obscenity and Pornography.* Vol. 8. Washington, D.C.: Government Printing Office, 1971.

Laing, R. D. *The Divided Self.* Baltimore: Penguin, 1965.

LeBoeuf, B. Male competition and reproductive success in elephant seals. *American Zoologist,* 1974, *14,* 163–76.

Lefcourt, H. M. The function of the illusions of control and freedom. *American Psychologist,* 1973, *28,* 417–25.

Liddell, H. S. The experimental neurosis. *Annual Review of Physiology,* 1947, *9,* 569–80.

Liddell, H. S. A comparative approach to the dynamics of experimental neurosis. *Annals of the New York Academy of Science,* 1953, *56,* 164–70.

Liebert, R. M., and Baron, R. A. Some immediate effects of televised violence on children's behavior. *Developmental Psychology,* 1972, *6,* 469–75.

Lindgren, H. C. Authoritarianism, independence, and child-centered practices in education: A study of attitudes. *Psychological Reports,* 1962, *10,* 747–50.

Lowry, R. J. *A. H. Maslow: An Intellectual Portrait.* Monterey, Calif.: Brooks/Cole, 1973.

MacKinnon, D. W. Personality and the realization of creative potential. In M. Bloomberg (ed.), *Creativity: Theory and Research.* New Haven: College and University Press, 1973.

Maslow, A. H. Dominance-feeling, personality and social behavior in women. *Journal of Social Psychology,* 1939, *10,* 3–39.

Maslow, A. H. A test for dominance-feeling (self-esteem) in women. *Journal of Social Psychology,* 1940, *12,* 255–70.

Maslow, A. H. Self-esteem (dominance feeling) and sexuality in women. *Journal of Social Psychology,* 1942, *16,* 259–94.

Maslow, A. H. *Motivation and Personality.* 2nd ed. New York: Harper and Row, 1970a.

Maslow, A. H. Psychological data and value theory. In A. H. Maslow (ed.), *New Knowledge in Human Values.* Chicago: Regnery, 1970b.

Maslow, A. H. *Religions, Values, and Peak-Experiences.* New York: Viking, 1970c.

Maslow, A. H. *The Farther Reaches of Human Nature.* New York: Viking, 1972.

Masserman, J. H. *Behavior and Neurosis.* Chicago: University of Chicago Press, 1943.

Masters, R. E. L., and Houston, J. *The Varieties of Psychedelic Experiences.* New York: Dell, 1966.

Masters, W. H., and Johnson, V. *Human Sexual Response.* Boston: Little, Brown, 1966.

Masters, W. H., and Johnson, V. *Human Sexual Inadequacy.* Boston: Little, Brown, 1970.

Mathes, E. W. The effects of physical attractiveness and anxiety on heterosexual attraction over a series of five encounters. *Journal of Marriage and the Family,* 1975, *37,* 769–73.

Mathes, E. W. Self-actualization, metavalues, and creativity. *Psychological Reports,* 1978, *43,* 215–22.

Mathes, E. W., and Edwards, L. L. An empirical test of Maslow's theory of motivation. *Journal of Humanistic Psychology,* 1978a, *18,* 75–77.

Mathes, E. W., and Edwards, L. L. Physical attractiveness as an input in social exchanges. *The Journal of Psychology,* 1978b, *98,* 267–75.

Mathes, E. W., and Guest, T. A. Anonymity and group antisocial behavior. *The Journal of Social Psychology,* 1976, *100,* 257–62.

Mathes, E. W., and Kahn, A. Diffusion of responsibility and extreme behavior. *Journal of Personality and Social Psychology.* 1975, *31,* 881–86.

May, R. The origins and significance of the existential movement in psychology. In R. May, E. Angel, and H. F. Ellenberger (eds.), *Existence*. New York: Basic Books, 1958.

May, R. *Love and Will*. New York: Dell, 1973.

McCasland, S. V. , Cairns, G. E., and Yu, D. C. *Religions of the World*. New York: Random House, 1969.

McClelland, D. C. *The Achieving Society*. Princeton: Van Nostrand, 1961.

McClelland, D. C. *n* Achievement and entrepreneurship: A longitudinal study. *Journal of Personality and Social Psychology*, 1965, *1*, 389–92.

McClelland, D. C., Atkinson, J. W., Clark, R. A., and Lowell, E. L. *The Achievement Motive*. New York: Appleton-Century-Crofts, 1953.

McClelland, D. C., and Winter, D. G. *Motivating Economic Achievement*. New York: Free Press, 1969.

McFarland, R. L., Nelson, C. L., and Rossi, A. M. Prediction of participation in group psychotherapy from measures of intelligence and verbal behavior. *Psychological Reports*, 1962, *11*, 291–98.

Meer, S. J. Authoritarian attitudes and dreams. *Journal of Abnormal and Social Psychology*, 1955, *5*, 74–78.

Milgram, S. Behavioral study of obedience. *Journal of Abnormal and Social Psychology*, 1963, *69*, 371–78.

Mills, J., and Aronson, E. Opinion change as a function of the communicator's attractiveness and desire to influence. *Journal of Personality and Social Psychology*, 1965, *1*, 173–77.

Minor, C. A., and Neel, R. G. The relationship between achievement motive and occupational preference. *Journal of Counseling Psychology*, 1958, *5*, 39–43.

Mischel, W. Delay of gratification, need for achievement, and acquiescence in another culture. *Journal of Abnormal and Social Psychology*, 1961, *62*, 543–52.

Mischel, W. *Personality and Assessment*. New York: Wiley, 1968.

Moody, R. A., Jr. *Life after Life*. New York: Bantam, 1976.

Mukherjee, B. N., and Sinha, R. Achievement values and self-ideal discrepancies in college students. *Personality: An International Journal*, 1970, *1*, 275–301.

Murchland, B. (ed.). *The Meaning of the Death of God.* New York: Vintage, 1967.

Murray, H. A. *Explorations in Personality.* New York: Science Editions, 1962.

Nadler, E. B. Yielding, authoritarianisms, and authoritarian ideology regarding groups. *Journal of Abnormal and Social Psychology,* 1959, *58,* 408–10.

Neill, A. S. *Summerhill: A Radical Approach to Child Rearing.* New York: Hart, 1960.

Newman, H. H., Freeman, F. N., and Holzinger, K. J. *Twins: A Study of Heredity and Environment.* Chicago: University of Chicago Press, 1937.

O'Neill, N., and O'Neill, G. *Open Marriage.* New York: Avon Books, 1973.

Orlofsky, J. L., Marcia, J. E., and Lesser, I. M. Ego identity status and the intimacy versus isolation crisis of young adulthood. *Journal of Personality and Social Psychology.* 1973, *27,* 211–19.

Ornstein, R. E. *The Psychology of Consciousness.* San Francisco: Freeman, 1972.

Paul, G. L. *Insight Versus Desensitization in Psychotherapy.* Palo Alto: Stanford University Press, 1966.

Paul, G. L. Insight versus desensitization in psychotherapy two years after termination. *Journal of Consulting Psychology,* 1967, *31,* 109–18.

Pavlov, I. P. *Conditioned Reflexes.* London: Oxford University Press, 1927.

Perls, F. S. *Gestalt Therapy Verbatim.* Moab, Utah: Real People Press, 1969.

Perls, F. S. *In and Out the Garbage Pail.* Moab, Utah: Real People Press, 1969.

Pike, J. A. *The Other Side.* New York: Dell, 1969.

Rest, J. R. The hierarchical nature of moral judgment: A study of patterns of comprehension and preference of moral stages. *Journal of Personality,* 1973, *41.*

Rest, J., Cooper, D., Coder, R., Masanz, J., and Anderson, D. Judging the important issues in moral dilemmas—an objective measure of development. *Developmental Psychology,* 1974, *10,* 491–501.

Rest, J., Turiel, E., and Kohlberg, L. Level of moral development as a determinant of preference and comprehension of moral judgments made by others. *Journal of Personality,* 1969, *37,* 225–52.

Richter, C. P. The phenomenon of unexplained sudden death in animals and man. In W. H. Grant (ed.), *Physiological Basis of Psychiatry.* Springfield, Ill.: Charles C. Thomas, 1958.

Riesman, D., Denney, R., and Glazer, N. *The Lonely Crowd.* Garden City, N. Y.: Doubleday-Anchor, 1953.

Robinson, P. The measurement of achievement motivation. Unpublished doctoral dissertation, Oxford University, 1961.

Rogers, C. R. *On Becoming a Person: A Therapist's View of Psychotherapy.* Boston: Houghton Mifflin, 1961.

Rogers, C. R. *The Therapeutic Relationship and Its Impact: A Study of Psychotherapy with Schizophrenics.* Madison: University of Wisconsin Press, 1967.

Rogers, C. R. *Carl Rogers on Encounter Groups.* New York: Harper and Row, 1970.

Rogers, C. R. *Carl Rogers on Personal Power.* New York: Delacorte Press, 1977.

Rosen, B. C., and D'Andrade, R. The psycho-social origins of achievement motivation. *Sociometry,* 1959, *22,* 185–218.

Rotter, J. B., Chance, J. E., and Phares, E. J. (eds.). *Applications of a Social Learning Theory of Personality.* New York: Holt, Rinehart, and Winston, 1972.

Rudin, S. A. National motives predict psychogenic death rates 25 years later. *Science,* 1968, *160,* 901–3.

Ruma, E. H., and Mosher, D. L. Relationship between moral judgment and guilt in delinquent boys. *Journal of Abnormal Psychology,* 1967, *72,* 122–27.

Saltzstein, H. D., Diamond, R. M., and Belenky, M. Moral judgment level and conformity behavior. *Developmental Psychology,* 1972, *7,* 327–36.

Sanders, E. *The Family.* New York: Avon, 1972.

Schuartz, S. H., Feldman, K. A., Brown, M. E., and Heingartner, A. Some personality correlates of conduct in two situations of moral conflict. *Journal of Personality,* 1969, *37,* 41–57.

Schultz, D. *Theories of Personality.* Monterey, Calif.: Brooks/Cole, 1976.

Schutz, W. C. *Joy.* New York: Random House, 1969.

Sears, R. R., Maccoby, E. E., and Levin, H. *Patterns of Child Rearing.* Evanston, Ill.: Row, Peterson, 1957.

Seeman, M. On the meaning of alienation. *American Sociological Review,* 1959, *24,* 789–91.

Seligman, M. E. P. *Helplessness: On Depression, Development, and Death.* San Francisco: Freeman, 1975.

Sherif, M. *Social Interaction.* Chicago: Aldine, 1967.

Sigall, H., Page, R., and Brown, A. C. Effort expenditure as a function of evaluation and evaluator attractiveness. *Representative Research in Social Psychology,* 1971, *2,* 19–25.

Skinner, B. F. *Beyond Freedom and Dignity.* New York: Knopf, 1971.

Skodak, M., and Skeels, H. M. A final follow-up of one hundred adopted children. *Journal of Genetic Psychology,* 1949, *75,* 85–125.

Sosa, J. N. Vascular effects of frustration on passive and aggressive members of a clinical population. Unpublished masters thesis, Florida State University, 1968.

Sperry, R. W. Bridging science and values: A unifying view of mind and brain. *American Psychologist,* 1977, *32,* 237–45.

Spielberger, C. D., and Katzenmeyer, W. G. Manifest anxiety, intelligence, and college grades. *Journal of Consulting Psychology,* 1959, *23,* 278.

Stevenson, I. *Twenty Cases Suggestive of Reincarnation.* Charlottesville: University Press of Virginia, 1974.

Stewart, N. A.G.C.T. Scores of army personnel grouped by occupation. *Occupations,* 1947, *26,* 5–41.

Stone, L., and Hokanson, J. E. Arousal reduction via self-punitive behavior. *Journal of Personality and Social Psychology,* 1969, *12,* 72–79.

Sundberg, N. D., and Tyler, L. E. *Clinical Psychology.* New York: Appleton-Century-Crofts, 1962.

Tart, C. T. *States of Consciousness.* New York: Dutton, 1975.

Taylor, S. P. Aggressive behavior and physiological arousal as a function of provocation and the tendency to inhibit aggression. *Journal of Personality,* 1967, *35,* 297–310.

Taylor, S. P. Aggressive behavior as a function of approval motivation and physical attack. *Psychonomic Science,* 1970, *18,* 195–96.

Taylor, S. P., and Epstein, S. Aggression as a function of the interaction of the sex of the aggressor and the sex of the victim. *Journal of Personality.* 1967, *35,* 474–86.

Telfer, M. A., Baker, D., Clark, G. R., and Richardson, C. E. Incidence of gross chromosomal errors among tall criminal American males. *Science,* 1968, *159,* 1249–50.

Terman, L. M. (ed.), et al. *Mental and physical traits of a thousand gifted children.* Vol. 1. Palo Alto: Stanford University Press, 1925.

Terman, L. M., and Oden, M. H. *The Gifted Child Grows Up.* In L. M. Terman (ed.), *Genetic Studies of Genius.* Vol. 4. Palo Alto: Stanford University Press, 1947.

Terman, L. M., and Oden, M. H. *The Gifted Group at Mid-life: Thirty-Five Years' Follow-up of the Superior Child.* In L. M. Terman (ed.), *Genetic Studies of Genius.* Vol. 5. Palo Alto: Stanford University Press, 1959.

Turiel, E. An experimental test of the sequentiality of developmental stages in the child's moral judgments. *Journal of Personality and Social Psychology,* 1966, *3,* 611–18.

Ulrich, R. E. Pain as a cause of aggression. *American Zoologist,* 1966, *6,* 643–62.

Ulrich, R. E., and Azrin, N. H. Reflexive fighting in response to aversive stimulation. *Journal of Experimental Analysis of Behavior,* 1962, *5,* 511–20.

Walster, E., Aronson, V., Abrahams, D., and Rottmann, L. Importance of physical attractiveness in dating behavior. *Journal of Personality and Social Psychology,* 1966, *4,* 508–16.

Washburn, S., and Hamburg, D. The implications of primate research. In I. DeVore (ed.), *Primate Behavior: Field Studies of Monkeys and Apes.* New York: Holt, Rinehart, and Winston, 1965.

Watson, J. B. *Behaviorism.* 2nd ed. New York: Norton, 1930.

Watson, J. B., and Rayner, R. Conditioned emotional responses. *Journal of Experimental Psychology,* 1920, *3,* 1–14.

Watts, A. *In My Own Way.* New York: Vintage, 1973.

White, R. W. Motivation reconsidered: The concept of competence. *Psychological Review,* 1959, *66,* 297–333.

Winterbottom, M. R. The relationship of need for achievement to learning experiences in independence and mastery. In J. W. Atkinson (ed.), *Motives in Fantasy, Action, and Society.* Princeton: Van Nostrand, 1958.

Witkin, H. A., Lewis, H. B., Hertzman, M., Machover, K., Meissner, P. B., and Wapner, S. *Personality Through Perception.* New York: Harper and Row, 1954.

Witkin, H. A., Lewis, H. B., Hertzman, M., Machover, K., Meissner, P. B., and Wapner, S. *Psychological Differentiation.* New York: Halstead, 1974.

Wolpe, J. Experimental neurosis as learned behavior. *British Journal of Psychology,* 1952, *43,* 243–68.

Wolpe, J. Learning theory and "abnormal fixations." *Psychological Review,* 1953, *60,* 111–16.

Wolpe, J. *Psychotherapy by Reciprocal Inhibition.* Palo Alto: Stanford University Press, 1958.

Wortman, C. B., Panciera, L., Shusterman, L., and Hibscher, J. Attributions of causality and reactions to uncontrollable outcomes. *Journal of Experimental Social Psychology,* 1976, *12,* 301–16.

Zimbardo, P. The human choice. In W. Arnold and D. Levin (eds.), *Nebraska Symposium on Motivation.* Lincoln: University of Nebraska Press, 1969.

Index

NAME INDEX

SUBJECT INDEX